The Diary of
a Russian Priest

The Diary of a Russian Priest

ALEXANDER ELCHANINOV

Translated by Helen Iswolsky
English edition prepared by Kallistos Timothy Ware

With an introduction by Tamara Elchaninov
and a Foreword by Dimitri Obolensky

ST. VLADIMIR'S SEMINARY PRESS
CRESTWOOD, NEW YORK 10707
1982

Library of Congress Cataloging in Publication Data

El'chaninov, Aleksandr V., d. 1934.
   The diary of a Russian priest.

   Reprint. Originally published: London: Faber, 1967.
   1. Spiritual life—Orthodox Eastern authors.
2. El'chaninov, Aleksandr V., d. 1934.   I. Title.
BX382.E413   1982   248.4'8193   82-16795
ISBN 0-88141-000-4

THE DIARY OF A RUSSIAN PRIEST

© Copyright 1967

by

TAMARA ELCHANINOV

ISBN 0-88141-000-4

First published in 1967 by Faber and Faber Limited
3 Queen Square London.
Reprinted by Faber and Faber Limited in 1973

PRINTED IN THE UNITED STATES OF AMERICA
BY
ATHENS PRINTING COMPANY
NEW YORK, N. Y.

Foreword

THE notes that form the material of this book were written, mostly without thought of publication, in the nineteen-twenties and thirties by a Russian priest living in France. Their author, Father Alexander Elchaninov, possessed rare gifts as a teacher and spiritual director. His notes, assembled and edited by his wife after his death in 1934, and which have already seen several Russian editions, provide ample evidence of these gifts. Those who knew him, whether as a teacher or a friend, will perhaps agree that he gave the impression of being at the same time involved and detached: he was capable of the most attentive and warm-hearted concern for those who had entrusted themselves to his spiritual care; and yet there seemed to be in him a kind of inner aloofness whose roots, one may suspect, lay in the depth and loneliness of his spiritual life.

His involvement was not only with people. Yet behind his interest in literature, in religious and philosophical thought, and later in psychology and psychiatry, behind his love of nature—especially of mountain scenery—always his main concern was for the human person. It was this concern, probably no less than his Christian faith, that alienated him in his youth from the radical and Marxist movements of pre-Revolutionary Russia and brought him into close contact with the members of the 'Religious and Philosophical Society' of St. Petersburg, who helped to rekindle an interest in religion among some of Russia's educated élite, and whose activities were part of a wider cultural movement which transformed the country's literature and art between 1900 and 1910. It accounts, more obviously still, for his success as a schoolmaster during the momentous years that spanned the First World War, the October Revolution, and the Russian civil war; and it does much to explain his achievements as an exile in the south of France in nurturing in the children of the Russian émigré community a devotion to the Orthodox Church and to their native land and culture. It was here, in Nice, particularly after his ordination to the priesthood in 1926, that Father Elchaninov's gifts as a teacher were afforded full scope; and there must be many of his pupils and spiritual children, now scattered in different lands, who gratefully remember their gentle and scrupulous master.

Of Father Alexander's spiritual life and stature others have written with greater competence. Some of their judgements are cited in the introduction to this book, written by his wife. His notes above all have preserved a revealing, though necessarily incomplete, memorial of his inner life. We may safely assume that, had their author lived to edit them, he would have re-worded some passages, amplifying their sometimes elliptic brevity or removing their occasionally stark impression. And yet, despite its fragmentary character, this book has surely a coherence and a unity of its own. Its basic theme—the pursuit of the spiritual life—is treated in a manner both timeless and topical. The author's reflections on the need for self-examination and self-discipline, on the subtle dangers of pride, on the significance of pain, and on the importance of the liturgy as a focus of the Christian's life—to mention only a few of the central topics of this book—are rooted in the biblical and patristic tradition of his Church. Yet they are never offered in a conventional framework, they patently stem from personal experience, and they show a concern for the predicament of modern man. Although there is no attempt to minimize the severity of the demands made on those who would accept the Gospel teaching in its totality, there is much in this book that is radiant and joyful, not least in those passages where the author speaks with insight and profundity of the spiritual dimension of marriage and of the transcendental aspects of human love. And in the last resort, through his sometimes frighteningly clear-sighted analysis of the nature and power of sin, and through his anguished compassion for human suffering, one is made aware of the relevance of the belief proclaimed by the Church which he served with such loyalty and singleness of purpose: the belief that for him who above all things seeks the Kingdom of Heaven transfiguration begins in this life on earth.

DIMITRI OBOLENSKY

Contents

Introduction

THE author of this work never intended to have it published. It was planned as a book a short time after Father Alexander's death, so that his life's unfinished task should be in some way continued and confirmed. Compiled by his wife, the pages that follow contain some of the notes that he made for his own use, together with excerpts from his letters, several outlines for sermons, and a few thoughts jotted at random on scraps of paper found among his writings.

This book will prove, perhaps, of particular value to people of the present day who have come from secular life to religion and to the Church: for Father Elchaninov himself came to the priesthood through the gates of secular culture, after many years of educational and social work, in which he experienced to the full the tensions and difficulties of Russia's tragic destiny.

Alexander Elchaninov belonged to a family with a long military tradition. The founder of the line, a knight by the name of Alendrok, came from Lithuania in the fifteenth century, entering the service of the Prince of Moscow Basil II (1425–62). Father Alexander valued this intimate link with Russia's historic past, but by the time of his birth in 1881, nothing material survived from those far-off days; the family no longer possessed the lands which it had once owned.

At the early age of twelve, Alexander lost his father. The family lived on a pension, and the young Alexander gave lessons to pay for his brother's tuition as well as his own at school. Although he was not the eldest, he quickly took the place of the first-born in the family. It was in him that his mother and sister always found moral support, and he acted as the senior to his two brothers. This is all the more remarkable as his was the gentlest disposition in the family. At school he exercised the same influence over others: his former school-fellow, the late Professor Michael Karpovich of Harvard, said of him: 'It is hard for me to express how deeply I am indebted to him in my intellectual and spiritual development. I only know that fundamentally I owe more to him than to anyone else I have met in my life.'

Alexander managed to earn enough money to study history and philology at the University of St. Petersburg, and after taking his degree he was offered an assistantship in the history department. His university years coincided with a period of great cultural and religious ferment among the Russian intelligentsia. It was at this time that the 'Religious and Philosophical Society' was founded at St. Petersburg, the aim of which was defined by the poet Zinaida Gippius as 'the creation of an open cultural platform for the free discussion of topics of religious and philosophical interest'. Its meetings were attended regularly by the student Elchaninov, the youngest member of the group. The idea of just such a society had long been a dream which he cherished while still at school, and he had discussed it with his friends, Vladimir Ern (1881–1915), the future philosopher and professor at Moscow University, and Paul Florensky (1882–?1952), subsequently priest, philosopher, and theologian, who was to end his life in a Soviet concentration camp. At a much later date, when Z. Gippius met Father Alexander as a priest, she told him of the unforgettable impression produced by the young student who, even in those days, represented the 'voice of conscience' to so many of those whom he encountered.

During this same period he also moved in literary circles and was offered a friendly reception by the writers Rozanov and Merezhkovsky. He was a frequent visitor at Vyacheslav Ivanov's extraordinary flat, 'The Tower', where he always received a particularly warm welcome: here he met Anna Akhmatova (at that time still a young poet), Gumilyov and Kuzmin.

In this way, thanks to his many friends, he met the leaders of Russian culture on the highest level, during a decade (1900–10) when that culture had attained an extraordinary flowering. It was a decade marked by a great recovery of faith, by a movement towards the Church on the part of circles in the Russian intelligentsia which had long been alienated from religion. In this spiritual revival the young Alexander Elchaninov himself played an active part: his university years already foreshadow the way of his entire life.

The great theologian, Father Sergius Bulgakov (1871–1944), who was the young man's older friend and teacher, recalls these early years thus:

It was a time of secular pastoral work, of the preaching of the faith in a society that had run loose, carried away by godlessness and indifference. And he, the future priest, was already dedicated to this work of preaching long before his ordination. In this task of mustering spiritual forces against atheism and indifference, he was a constant labourer and collaborator, a humble and devoted worker, fulfilling all that was assigned to him. . . . To this task he brought his pastoral qualities, and the special charm of his youth. When he appeared, with his gentle, luminous look, people's hearts went out to him, and a smile appeared on their lips.

A particularly close friendship, and one that had started during his childhood, bound young Alexander Elchaninov to Paul Florensky. It was under Florensky's influence—and also from his own inclination—that Elchaninov gave up his promising university career at St. Petersburg and moved to Moscow, enrolling in the Theological Academy there, although he did not at that time consider the possibility of becoming a priest. He joined the newly-founded Moscow 'Society for the Study of Religion and

Philosophy', becoming its first secretary. About the same time his first articles began to appear in print in the review *Novy Put* ('The New Way'): first an essay on 'Speransky's Mysticism', and then, a year later, instalments of his book *The History of Religion*. He also took part in the attempts made during this period to overcome the traditional dependence of the Church on the Russian State, and in efforts to bring the social order closer to the ideals of the Gospel. In later life he used to recall how one night, in the woods close to a Moscow suburb, he read and explained the Gospel to a group of workers: for this he was fined one hundred roubles by the police who suspected him of subversive activities.

At the end of his first year Elchaninov's course at the Academy was interrupted: he was drafted into the army and sent to the Caucasus. He did not resume his theological studies. Quite apart from the question of military service, there was another reason for this: at the Academy he had been troubled by the theological approach underlying much of the teaching, an approach typical of many members of the higher clergy during the Synodal period of Russian Church history. As he put it in a letter to Florensky: 'Their positivism and nominalism, their attacks on the *imyaslavie*[1] and their hostility towards the Old Believers,[2] all show how limited is their mystical understanding.'

Thus exterior circumstances, combined with his own inability to accept the outlook prevailing at the Academy of those days, led him away from this path, notwithstanding all the efforts of his friend Florensky to hold him back. Florensky himself felt the same misgivings, but he persevered with the course, eventually receiving the degree of Doctor of Theology from the Academy,

---

[1] The teaching developed by a section of the monks in the Russian monastery on Mount Athos, according to which God is mystically present in His Name.

[2] Russian sect dating from the seventeenth century, strongly conservative and nationalistic, but representing much that was best in the Russian Orthodox tradition. Their members split from the main body of the Russian Church because they refused to accept certain liturgical changes.

after gaining a moral victory by successfully defending his thesis on 'Spiritual Truth'. This was published in 1914 under the title *The Pillar and the Ground of Truth*, a work of considerable importance in the development of modern Russian theology.

In 1908, at the end of his military service in the Caucasus, Elchaninov remained in Tiflis and took up educational work in a private school of an entirely new type. The founder of this school, General Levandovsky (his future father-in-law), in virtue of his high military rank and thanks to the Emperor's personal approval, had succeeded in setting up an establishment utterly unlike any previously known in Russia. It was a co-educational school with a widely-ranging programme of study, allowing an important place to sport and gymnastics, while its regulations permitted the pupils a large measure of self-government. Its spirit of liberty and constructive attitude to questions of discipline attracted Alexander Elchaninov, and he was greatly inspired by the creative possibilities which such a school offered. He started as teacher of literature and psychology and later, during the years 1914–20, held the position of principal. In 1918 he married the daughter of the school's founder.

A former pupil, Mrs. Militsa Zernov, recalls his work at the school in these words:

The school enlisted the most gifted teachers, but among them all Alexander Elchaninov was talented to a quite exceptional and incomparable degree. His teaching carried into effect, more than anything else, the institution's main idea—to be a school of joy, creativity, and freedom. The curriculum did not conform to any fixed pattern and passed beyond the limits of every programme. We, who were Alexander Elchaninov's pupils, have kept many happy personal memories of our time at the school, and most of all we recall the charm of our teacher's personality.

Already, as a schoolmaster, Elchaninov was a true spiritual director, 'a priest even before his priesthood', in the words of Father Bulgakov.

During this period Elchaninov lectured at special courses for women on the History of Religions, and gave a series of addresses on the theme especially close to his heart—the new Russian religious and philosophical thought and its leaders, all of whom he knew personally. These lectures proved such a success that he and his friend, another headmaster, G. N. Gehtman, thought of following them up by establishing a religious-philosophical faculty within the Universities of Moscow and St. Petersburg. This idea met with general approval, plans were prepared, and lists of possible directors drawn up: but war and revolution put an end to all this preliminary work.

The Bolshevik régime, which did not come to power in the Caucasus until 1920, deprived Elchaninov of his post as principal. The school was nationalized and—paradoxically—all the liberal and advanced aspects of the curriculum were abolished by the revolutionary government. During the months of famine and chaos that ensued, Elchaninov worked in the American Near East Relief, organizing crafts, workshops, sports and educational recreation for children who were fed by the Hoover Relief Organization.

Like so many other members of the intelligentsia Elchaninov was driven from his native land by the tempest of revolution. In 1921 he left Russia with his wife and baby daughter, settling in the south of France at Nice. Here he undertook agricultural work at first, at the same time giving lessons in Russian language and history to Russian children studying at French schools. He gave lectures on a variety of topics to the Russian colony, and organized religious and philosophical discussion groups for the Russian youth. His house soon became a centre where many intellectual leaders of the emigration could be found, on a visit from Paris—professors and writers such as Bulgakov, Vysheslavtsev, Zander, Ilyin, and many others.

But by now it had become clear that an ordinary career as a teacher could no longer satisfy Alexander, and that he was called to another, higher vocation. Here is his own account of how his path became clear to him:

> I received a letter from Father Sergius B. (Bulgakov) in which he urgently advised me to enter the priesthood. I was dumbfounded. At first I was frightened, as we are when we hear the voice of destiny, of fate. I understood immediately that this was something irrevocable, that this was indeed my destiny. If it had been anything else, perhaps I would have tried to avoid it; but over this I scarcely hesitated—I went out to meet it, and then I felt an immense joy and clarity in my soul. Along the old path—education, lecturing—there was no longer anything for me to live for; along this new path, I feel revived and reborn. This is my initiation to the second degree. The first degree was marriage, the second is priesthood.

And further:

> I have always been frightened, and especially during the last year, by the swift passing of time; this was because I myself was not moving. Now, having decided to enter the priesthood, I have moved drastically against time: or—to put it more correctly—I have plunged into the very depths, where time is irrelevant.

Speaking of Elchaninov's decision to become a priest, and of the other careers which he might have followed, Father Bulgakov observes:

> What might his fate have been, what might he have become in future years? According to our human understanding, and judging by the serious basis and scientific method we find in all his works, we might answer that he could have become a professor, a scholar. If he had continued in those literary circles in which he moved in his youth, he might have become a writer and editor. But all these possibilities faded away from force of circumstances. His work in education might have been still further developed, and perhaps he would have made some brilliant discovery in this field. It was suggested at one point

that he should lecture at the Orthodox Theological Institute in Paris, but in that case he would have had to submit to the rules of systematic theology. This, however, did not happen, nor should it be regretted. It should rather be considered a godsend, for his ordination to the priesthood led him to discover his highest gift and true vocation—that of a priest, a pastor of souls, confessor and teacher. Every man is called to realize his highest gift: it was priesthood that revealed to the highest degree Father Alexander's interior strength and his power over human hearts.

Entry to the priesthood in 1926 meant for Alexander Elchaninov the natural continuation both of his inner development and of his outward activity. More than that—in priesthood he discovered what he was really called to be, realizing God's design for himself. One of his friends said about his physical appearance on the day of his ordination: 'All his icon-like features seemed at last to have found their true image.' Priesthood gave new inspiration to his whole life. 'Before priesthood', he wrote a year after his ordination, 'there was so much I had to be silent about, holding myself back. Priesthood, for me, means the possibility of speaking with a full voice.'

Describing his feelings during those first days of his ministry, Father Alexander wrote:

I feel calm and serene—often happy, almost in bliss. I know a firm hand is leading me. This was clear to me even before my ordination and particularly during the ordination itself; and it is still so at present. And have I not been blessed by many miracles? Was it not miraculous that I became a priest? My ordination took place in exceptional circumstances, helped by the general good will of my friends, encouraged by my wife's full consent and approval, and upheld by Father Sergius' good counsel.

And again:

What joy to be a priest! Priesthood is the only profession in which people always show you their most earnest side, and you yourself live in earnest all the time.

Father Alexander's interests were primarily moral, ascetic, and practical in character, rather than abstract and theological. His attention was centred on the human soul, on the application of Christianity to life. In his priestly work he concentrated especially on the work of hearing confessions and giving spiritual direction. 'Confession', Mother Maria[1] has said, 'was his priesthood's essential calling. It is significant that the first symptoms of his fatal illness struck him down while he was hearing confessions.' Many testimonies survive, showing what kind of confessor he was and what he meant to his penitents. 'For me he was the incarnation of God's truth on earth. I knew no one who was better, clearer, simpler, and wiser. Thanks to my contacts with him, the shortest way to God was revealed to me. . . . How often the very thought that it would be necessary to tell him about it in confession was enough to keep me from sin.' 'His direction and instruction are sometimes almost imperceptible, he is sparing in words, but each one of them, so full of human understanding, leaves a mark for life.' 'He had the gift of attention and of charity for everyone, and the gift of self-forgetfulness—therein lay his inner strength and the secret of his extraordinary influence on people.'

Another part of his priestly ministry that lay close to his heart was the task of preaching. Just as his previous instructions in class and his lectures had been deeply spiritual, so now his preaching was marked by clarity and conciseness. Each word was saturated with thought. It was his custom to prepare *what* he had to say but not *how* he would say it: this gave his sermons a sense of a spontaneity and deep conviction, combined with clear thought.[2]

---

[1] Mother Maria (Skobtsova) (1891–1945), Russian Orthodox nun dedicated to corporal works of mercy, distinguished as an author and poet; died in the Nazi concentration camp at Ravensbrück.

[2] Compare what Father Alexander himself says about the preparation of his sermons on p. 220.

Fullness of heart and great simplicity endowed his words with an extraordinary power. One of the leaders at a summer camp gives us this example:

Father Alexander is giving a talk in the camp, closely surrounded by a circle of listeners. Their faces have suddenly changed, becoming serious and alert. The theme of the talk is a difficult spiritual and ascetic problem; it is remarkable at times how girls who appear utterly frivolous and hopelessly immature in the eyes of their leaders can develop such a deep and engrossing interest in Father Alexander's words. When he arrives, he gradually transfigures the entire spirit of the camp and performs miracles.

In his youth work, Father Alexander was actively associated with the Russian Student Christian Movement, to which he had already been attracted in Russia before the Revolution. 'I value the "Movement" more and more', he wrote, 'as the meeting ground of all that is alive in the Church, of all those who accept Christianity not as a tradition, not as mere words or a way of life, but as life itself.' He was especially inspired by the large annual conventions of the Movement: 'The atmosphere of the Movement's conventions reminds me a little of the fire and intimacy of Christian communities in apostolic days, when the Spirit blew and miracles occurred—for without the Spirit a Christian cannot breathe and is only a shadow, the mere skeleton of a Christian.' A former pupil who met him at one of these conventions remarked: 'He is still the same familiar teacher, but there is a new depth in him.'

His spiritual director, Father Sergius Bulgakov, gives this evaluation of Father Alexander as a priest: 'He represented a combination of two things: first, a humble devotion to Orthodoxy, the simplicity of a childlike faith; and secondly, the full intellectual refinements of the Russian cultural tradition.' Others who knew him as a priest speak similarly of his simplicity, and also of his humility and lightheartedness. 'The wisdom of humility, the wisdom of meekness gave him a special power over souls.' 'The most essential thing is his simplicity. Not the primitive simplicity of a man unacquainted with the world's complexity, but a far-seeing simplicity that has taken the measure of that very complexity.' 'When I saw him as a priest, I defined to myself his special attributes: a high spiritual exaltation, combined with a joyfulness which at times seemed almost lighthearted.'

Besides his work as a priest, there was also his life in the family, in the circle of his wife, his son and two daughters: but of this it is difficult for me, as his wife, to speak. I will content myself with quoting the remarks of two friends: 'In his home the warmth of family life was blended with the highest ideals and interests.' 'One glance at his home life was enough to show where lay his joy and happiness.' And another friend wrote at the time of his death: 'Father Alexander's time and energy were entirely devoted to God and to his fellow men. And God demanded of him the final sacrifice, that of his life, which meant parting with what was dearest to him on earth—his family.'

Perhaps because of his lightheartedness, Father Alexander's entire person preserved an extraordinary youthfulness. In the words of his father-in-law:

Was there the least sign of advancing age in him? Not only did he remain unchanged, but he seemed to grow younger and younger at heart. Even physically you would scarcely say that this was a man who had reached the fiftieth year of a life of hard work, always filled with activities beyond his strength, which yet never distracted him from his intense inner life.

But he died comparatively early, at the age of fifty-three, when still seemingly full of vigour and new plans. He had just been transferred from Nice to the Russian Cathedral in Paris. In the summer of 1934 he was taken to hospital with a perforated ulcer of the stomach. A tragic fate, so it seemed, pursued him: several medical mistakes, carelessness and inefficiency in hospitals, and fatal misunderstandings during the treatment, appeared to be leading him inexorably to his death, despite all the efforts to save him. He passed away in great suffering during August 1934, leaving behind him a wife with three small children, the eldest fourteen and the youngest eight.

Father Alexander's life work is movingly summed up by Mother Maria:

> For those who knew Father Alexander there could be no doubt about 'the great destiny' which was his. He was a representative of that highly cultured stratum in Russian society which determined the spiritual character and the ideas of the brilliant period marking the beginning of the twentieth century. In his earthly path among us, I would venture to claim, Father Alexander displayed the perfect fullness of humble Christian sanctity. After many years of brilliant educational work, after entering into all the refined complexities of Russian religious and philosophical thought, he attained to a wise, mature, humble, and simple priesthood. Such were our thoughts of his 'great destiny' at the time of his death. There in the coffin, clothed in golden vestments, with a large bronze cross clasped in his hands, his calm, meek features sealed by higher wisdom, lay a man who had disclosed and realized himself before God and before his fellow men, a man who had proved that the road from Athens may, even in our own time, lead a soul to the heavenly Jerusalem.

Such was the personality of Father Alexander Elchaninov, as it appeared to his family and friends. But perhaps this personality is even more fully and directly reflected in this book: brief and fragmentary though it is, we can hear his own living voice speaking to us.

Being composed of random notes, the book naturally does not represent every aspect of Father Alexander's character. Most of his notes are concerned with ascetic themes and with problems of the spiritual life, and as a result they may convey a certain impression of severity, which was not in fact at all characteristic of him. He was, on the contrary, lighthearted and full of radiant joy, indulgent towards the faults of others, natural and spontaneous, with a subtle irony and humour.

Two chapters in this book stand somewhat on their own, for they constitute the first stages of books which Father Alexander hoped some day to write. Not long before his last illness, he said that he would like to compose a work specially designed for young people, to answer the many questions put to him that were typical of modern youth. He kept a file, inscribed 'Letters to Young People', but he did not live to complete this plan. Extracts from the material which he collected form one chapter in the present book. Another chapter, 'Advice to Young Priests', is similar in origin. This section, too, contains only a few scattered notes, but their theme was very close to Father Alexander's heart, and he intended to prepare a special book on this subject also.

Apart from these chapters, planned by the author himself, the rest of the material is presented without any systematic order; this has been done deliberately, so as not to offer any interpretation that might stand between the reader and the author. Each reader is left free to discover for himself, according to his own needs, what was the essence of Father Alexander's spiritual image.

What is published here represents unfortunately no more than a small portion of what he actually wrote. Nearly all his early writings were left behind in Russia at the time of the revolution—for we only expected to be abroad for a short while—and they had to be destroyed by his relatives during the period of the terror. Many of the other papers were lost during the second world war: they were deposited for safe keeping in a special place, but this was discovered and plundered during the German occupation. Part of the documents were recovered in a remarkable way: a German soldier, happening to meet a Russian woman, handed her a parcel containing Father Alexander's photographs. 'These must be very precious to someone,' he said, 'and perhaps you can find the owner.' The photographs were indeed returned to the family, but several notebooks which had been with them had disappeared.

Fragmentary though they are, Father Alexander's notes have spoken directly to men's hearts. Despite the limited resources of the Russian emigration, three Russian editions have already appeared, and extracts have also been published in English translation. Father Alexander's words have not only been read by many thousands of his fellow-countrymen in exile, but they have even reached those behind the Iron Curtain. 'It is impossible', says a letter received from the Baltic States under Communist rule, 'to reckon the multitude of souls in this country brought to the faith by Father Alexander's book. It is passed on from one person to another and copied by hand'. The writer Michael Koryakov quotes Father Elchaninov's own words: 'There are no casual encounters: either God sends us those we need, or, without our knowledge, we ourselves are sent to others by His will.' And Koryakov adds: 'I truly believe that Father Alexander Elchaninov's book has been sent by God to the world, not to us Russians alone, who have the joy of reading it in the original version, but to the whole of humanity, for such a book should be translated into many languages.'

Such, then, is the present book—not a literary work, but an authentic document of human life, reflecting the author's soul. For those who knew Father Elchaninov and were devoted to him it will provide a few landmarks, enabling them to recall the characteristics of their beloved pastor and once more to hear his voice. To those who did not know him it will perhaps serve as a confirmation and a support: in other words it will do exactly what Father Alexander did for others all his life.

TAMARA ELCHANINOV (ELTCHANINOFF)

Fragments of a Diary

BEFORE I became a priest there was so much I had to be silent about, holding myself back. Priesthood, for me, means the possibility of speaking with a full voice.

†

There is no consolation for suffering except to consider it against the background of the 'other world'. And this, indeed, is fundamentally the only correct point of view. If this world alone exists, then everything in it is absolute nonsense: separation, sickness, innocent suffering, death. But all these acquire a meaning in that ocean of life which invisibly washes the small island of our earthly being. Which of us has not experienced the breath of other worlds in dreams, in prayer? When a man finds in himself the power to acquiesce in the ordeal sent him by God, he achieves great progress in his spiritual life.

†

To be a philosopher is not the same as to be a theologian. 'If you truly pray, you are a theologian' (Evagrius of Pontus).[1] Inner perfection is necessary in order to understand what is perfect.

†

---

[1] Greek ascetic and spiritual writer (346–99).

What is this continual sense of dissatisfaction, of anxiety, which we normally feel within us, save the stifled voice of conscience speaking to us inwardly on the subconscious level, and often contradicting our own will and declaring the untruth that our life is? As long as we live in conflict with the law of light which has been granted us, this voice will not be silent, for it is the voice of God Himself in our soul. On the other hand, that rare feeling of keen satisfaction, of plenitude and joy, is the happiness caused by the union of the divine principle in our soul with the universal harmony and the divine essence of the world.

†

Why is every 'delectation', every 'sweetness', a sin? Because the moment of delectation marks the strengthening of our personal sensations; the more intense the delectation, the greater is our break with the universal harmony around us. Delectation leads to self-love, self-love to the disintegration of harmony, and disintegration to death.

†

What hinders us most from answering the calls of the Church? Being taken up with *our own*, holding on to *our own*. It makes little difference whether it is something good or bad: it is *mine*. And this goes on from the first dawning of consciousness until death.

†

'It is dangerous to swim when fully dressed, and it is dangerous, when carried away by passions, to investigate the mysteries of the Godhead' (*The Ladder*).[1] But this does not mean (as many imagine)

---

[1] *The Ladder of Divine Ascent*, the work of a monk of Sinai, St. John Climacus (seventh century): one of the most famous of Greek ascetic writings.

that we should not engage in theology at all; it means that we must free ourselves from our enslavement to the passions, and we will then have a glimpse of the 'mysteries of the Godhead'.

†

I am continually pondering the text: 'If ye were of the world, the world would love his own' (John xv. 19). Our sufferings are the sign that we belong to Christ; and the greater they are, the more evident it is that we are not 'of the world'. Why did all the saints, following the example of Christ Himself, suffer so much? Contact with the world, being plunged into the midst of things, gives pain to the followers of Christ; only the children of this world suffer no pain. This is a kind of unerring chemical reaction.

†

However just and pure a man may be, there is always an element of sin in him which cannot enter the Kingdom of God and which must be burned up. Our sins are burned up by our sufferings.

†

What augments our spiritual forces? A temptation which has been overcome.

†

The presence within us finite beings of the infinite—of love—leads us to long for death as an entrance into the Infinite.

†

Even in this our dark life God does not forsake us, but He is with us in our prayer, in the sacraments, in our love of God. The love of God proves His communion with us.

†

Life is a precious and unique gift, and we squander it foolishly and carelessly, forgetful of its brevity.

Either we look back with yearning on the past or else we live in the expectation of a future in which, it seems to us, life will really begin; whereas the present—that is, our life as it actually is— is wasted in these fruitless dreams and regrets.

†

The opinion of others about us—this is the mirror before which we all, almost without exception, pose. A man moulds himself in order to be such as he wishes to appear to others. But the real man, as he actually is, remains unknown to all, often himself included, while what acts and lives is a figure invented and dressed up by his own imagination. This tendency to deceive is so great that, distorting his very nature, a man will sacrifice his own self— the unique and inimitable element present in every human personality.

But how great is the attraction we feel whenever we meet a person free of this cancer, and how much we love the complete simplicity and directness of children, who have not as yet entered the realm of self-consciousness! Yet we have the alternative of struggling consciously to return from this evil complexity to simplicity. In any case, when we become aware of the presence of this evil in us, the task is already half accomplished.

†

What joy to be a priest! Yesterday I heard the confessions of an
28

entire family. The children especially were most lovable – two boys of about seven or eight. All the evening I was almost rapt in ecstasy. Priesthood is the only profession in which men show you the most earnest side of their nature, in which you also live 'in earnest' all the time.

†

The Apostle says, 'I have begotten you' (1 Cor. iv. 15), 'I travail in birth again until Christ be formed in you' (Gal. iv. 19). The Apostles possessed indeed this most wonderful gift of taking upon themselves the process of generation and giving birth to new souls, new personalities. The converts who were thus endowed with a new personality welcomed this gift as something highly desirable, for which they had pined and hoped.

†

However weak and sinful we are, taken as individuals, it is such a joy to feel that for all of us only one thing is needful.

†

'Unto the Jews I became as a Jew, that I might gain the Jews. . . . To them that are without law, as without law. . . . To the weak became I as weak. . . . I am made all things to all men, that I might by all means save some' (1 Cor. ix. 20–22). This is the inscription on the grave of *starets* Amvrosy,[1] and it is also the tactics which I myself adopt unconsciously.

†

---

[1] Starets Amvrosy (1812–91), monk at the Optina Hermitage in Russia, celebrated as a spiritual director.

The title *starets* (plural, *startsy*) means literally an 'elder': it is applied to a monk (occasionally a lay person) distinguished for his saintliness, long experience in the spiritual life, and gift for guiding souls.

In my relationship with others, I should like to plunge deep into every situation, entering the very soul of each person who comes to me, speaking to him as if he were the person most dear to me in the entire world. But where are we to find a love so great as to embrace everyone? How are we to love the foolish, the conceited who fuss over their mean little futilities, when (to make it worse) we are convinced that paying them attention only does them harm? I suppose that each of us needs to be a saint in order to grasp, through the thick layer of deposited rubbish, the element in each person which is unique and cannot ever be repeated—his soul—and to address that alone.

†

The proud man is deaf and blind to the world; he does not see the world, but only himself reflected in everything.

†

How shall we comfort those who weep? By weeping with them.

†

Conversation with X after an operation for cancer. She feels constant, terrible pain ('like dogs gnawing and tearing me to pieces'), and there is no hope at all of any improvement in her situation. Here are her thoughts: 'I think that I understand why God has sent us this misfortune. We are so bogged down in daily trifles, in petty anger, irritation, that God wanted to shake us. How everything has been changed, what extraordinary spiritual qualities have been revealed in all of us! Yesterday L. spent the night with me, and what a night! She was infinitely gentle and patient, she did everything so quietly, so skilfully. And everyone has been so kind and attentive.' Here, then, is the meaning of

30

suffering. Our Lord has infinite pity for us, but what is to be done if it is only when stricken by misfortune and calamity that we are able to give out some sort of sparks, some sort of sacred fire? That is why there are wars, revolutions, sickness. All this seemed far more full of meaning yesterday, in a dying person's room, than it appears in these pallid notes.

†

All that is sinful in us is so much alive, so full-blooded, that our usual feeble penitence is completely disproportionate to this sinful element that possesses us.

†

To turn our gaze on the image of heavenly beauty–this is the best means of freeing ourselves from the captivity of hell and of resisting its suggestions.

†

From dialogues with myself:
—Why do you not give some thought to this? It is so very important.
—That is precisely my way of thinking about important things. Put the whole machine in order, and then the answer will emerge automatically. 'Take no thought how or what thing ye shall answer' (Luke xii. 11).

†

It often seems to me that the thorns and thistles on our life's course are ordained by God in order to cure specifically *our* soul. I see this with absolute clearness in my personal life.

†

In confession, a feeble memory is no excuse: forgetfulness is caused by inattention, a lack of earnestness, by hardness and indifference to sin. A sin whose weight *presses on the soul* cannot be forgotten.

†

I have observed an almost universal indifference during confession, especially among men. I thank God that He nearly always lets me experience confession as a catastrophe.

†

People generally have a habit of not mentioning sins against the seventh commandment, as if this was something that did not concern confession: 'It's my own private affair.' Many who are involved in an illicit liaison do not mention it, regarding it as something quite natural.

†

In confession the most important thing is the state of soul in the person making the confession, regardless of who the confessor may be. It is *your* confession that matters, and not the confessor who speaks to you. But we often make the mistake of putting first the personality of the priest who hears the confession.

†

If you are seized with anger towards someone, try to imagine that both you and he must die. How insignificant his fault will then appear, and how unjust your anger, even if formally justified.

†

Obstacles to prayer: weak, incorrect, and insufficient faith;

too much agitation, bustle, absorption in worldly affairs; sinful, impure, angry feelings and thoughts.

†

Sickness is the most favourable time for us to return to our own heart, to God. As soon as our health has improved, the possibility of doing this recedes once more to an infinite distance.

†

If a person has chosen the path of perfection and follows Christ, the unique value of this path becomes clear to him, and absolutely convincing from within. Those who have entered this path are few, yet there are practically none who, having chosen it, afterwards turn back. According to Christ's promise, he that seeks shall find.

†

Faith has nothing to fear from negative polemics, from the ordeal by the mind; faith is able to withstand such an ordeal. But what it has to fear is the weakness of our spirit, 'the apostasy of the heart' (Kireevsky's expression).[1]

†

Those who demand proofs in order to believe are on the wrong track. Faith is a free choice; wherever there is a desire for proof, even a desire hidden from ourselves, there is no faith. The evidences of divine manifestation must not be taken as 'proofs'— this would be to degrade and nullify the great virtue of faith.

†

---

[1] Ivan Kireevsky (1806–56), Russian religious thinker and writer, a leading member of the Slavophile movement.

The sense of deep sinfulness experienced by saints is caused by their nearness to the source of light–to Christ.

†

To free ourselves from inner chaos, we must recognize objective order.

†

How difficult is our approach to God, especially in the case of some of us, when everything–even nature, heredity, and the entire composition of man–builds up a wall between him and God.

The kind of man we most often encounter presents a combination of three traits: (1) pride–faith in his own strength, delight in his own creations; (2) a passionate love of earthly life; and (3) the absence of any sense of sin. How can such men approach God? As they now are, they are hopelessly isolated from God; they do not even feel the need of Him. And this is precisely the kind of personality that is developed in the conditions of modern life, through education, literature and so on. The idea of God is erased from the soul. What catastrophes are required, before such a man can be reborn!

†

Three series of impressions: reading the Gospel about the Gadarene swine; observing a madman in the cathedral; reading the chapter on evil and freedom in Berdyaev's *The Destiny of Man*:[1] 'Freedom was not created by God, it is primary and without a beginning.' Thus responsibility for the freedom of the creature is removed from God the Creator. Man is at the same time a child of God and a child of chaos (freedom); non-being freely agreed to become being, but at the same time it turned aside from the true

---

[1] Nikolai Berdyaev (1874–1948), religious thinker and writer, a prominent member of the Russian intelligentsia in Paris after the Revolution.

path into hell and chaos. This is the source of sin and madness—chaotic self-will instead of a voluntary and free submission to the law of light. 'I am come that they might have life, and that they might have it more abundantly.' (John x. 10.)

†

There is a type of spirituality closely enmeshed with the emotions—aesthetic, sentimental, passionate—which can easily coexist with selfishness, vanity, and sensuality. Men of this type seek the praise and the good opinion of their spiritual father; it is a very hard task for him to hear and accept their confession, for they come in order to complain of others, to whimper; they are full of themselves and readily accuse their neighbour. The poor quality of their religious devotion is best demonstrated by the ease with which they pass into a state of anger and irritation. They are further from the possibility of genuine contrition than the most inveterate sinners.

†

A constant reproach addressed to Christians: 'Your faith has no outward effect on your way of life. If you really believed in such marvellous and astonishing things, you would live in a different way.'

Answer: 'Surely you believe that death is inevitable? Not only do you believe this but you know it for certain. And yet, does it make any great difference to your way of life? None at all.'

†

If a man does not order his life according to logic and common sense but follows the supreme law—the law of love—then he is always right. All other laws are as nothing compared with love, which not only directs men's hearts, but 'moveth the sun and other stars.'[1] He who keeps this law within himself lives. He who lets himself be governed by philosophy, politics, and reason alone, dies.

†

Faith originates in love; love, in contemplation. It is impossible not to love Christ. If we saw Him now, we should not be able to take our eyes off Him, we should 'listen to him in rapture'; we should flock round Him as did the multitudes in the Gospels. All that is required of us is not to resist. We have only to yield to Him, to the contemplation of His image—in the Gospels, in the saints, in the Church—and He will take possession of our hearts.

†

Why is it so important to read the Lives of the Saints?—In the infinite spectrum of the paths leading to God, which are revealed in the lives of the various saints, we can discover our own; we can obtain guidance to help us emerge from the jungle in which we have become entangled through our human sinfulness, and so gain access to the path which leads towards the light.

†

What should we say to a dying woman who does not suspect the approach of death; who tells us in her perplexity, 'I am ready neither for life nor for death'? It is impossible for us to lead a genuine and dignified life in this world unless we prepare ourselves for death, unless we continually meditate on death and eternal life.

†

---

[1] 'L'amor che muove il sol e l'altre stelle' (Dante, *The Divine Comedy*).

Death, the thing which man dreads most of all, holds no terrors for the believer, just as abysses, precipices, and falls hold no terrors for winged creatures.

†

A rule of life: to change my residence only when circumstances force me to do so; to undertake nothing in the practical sphere on my own initiative, but to delve deeply into the earth on the spot where God has placed me.

†

How pathetic is our satisfaction with this present life! The fragile little island of our 'normal' existence will be washed completely away in the worlds beyond the tomb.

†

Advice to the family of the dead: to turn away our feeling and our pain from the flesh which will sink into the earth; not to let ourselves be tortured by the memory of earthly feelings and of earthly joys linked to the dead, but to step together with the dead —if only mentally—into that other world; to let ourselves be comforted by the love of those who are dear to us and by praying together with them; to let our nerves and body rest.

†

The difference between Job and his friends. Job is an honest, truthful man, who wants facts not words. The others are people concerned with religious talk, shibboleths, traditional formulas. Job cries out against falsehood, against the incomprehensibility of suffering, the prosperity of sinners and the torments of all the innocent – not only his own. His friends answer him with vague and misleading phrases; to them, everything is clear; and having established an orderly scheme in word and thought, they imagine that they have established harmony in the outside world as well. This type of man is found all too often and in every walk of life, including the clergy and scholars.

†

There is a certain 'inhibited' condition of the soul in which we find it difficult to smile; we feel no softness or tenderness towards anyone – our state is one of petrified insensibility. Only prayer, especially the prayer of the Church, will dispel this condition. Such a mood is habitual to the proud, the melancholy, the vain, the debauched, the miserly; but to a certain degree it is inherent in men in general: it is the condition of sin, of the absence of grace – man's common condition. So far as the soul is concerned, this is already hell on earth, death despite the life of the body; and it is the natural consequence of sin, which literally *kills* the soul.

†

'How hardly shall they that have riches enter into the kingdom of God' (Luke xviii. 24). It is not only material riches that prevent us from entering the kingdom of God; a still greater obstacle are the higher endowments of the mind – talents, special abilities, will-power. How difficult not to be carried away by all these, not to fall into vanity and pride.

†

The normal order within our soul:
(1) A mysterious inner life of the spirit of which we are un-aware, the genuine pledge of our salvation – given to us through

Holy Baptism, through the sacraments, through the inspiration of the Holy Ghost.

(2) The mist of our pseudo-virtues, disfigured and corroded by the acid of vainglory: our so-called good deeds, our so-called prayer, truthfulness, and honesty. This mist obscures the true and pathetic picture of our soul and hinders our contrition.

(3) The clouds of the actual sins which we do not remember, which we easily forgive ourselves: our continual censure of other men, mockery, contempt, indifference, coldness, anger.

(4) Lastly, beneath all this, the deep, ancient strata of hereditary corruption which we share with the whole of humanity— the fundamental sins from which arise, like poisonous vapours, blasphemous thoughts and impulses, all kinds of impurities, monstrous perversions. . . .

†

I think of the purifying and sanctifying value of sweat, tears, and blood—of toil, contrition, martyrdom. Through them the body is freed of its psychic and animal elements, and the spiritual principle, meeting no obstacle, pervades the whole man. That is why the Church exalts its martyrs, emphasizing precisely the shedding of blood; and that is why people honour the dead killed in war.

†

We must dwell in constant communion with that part of contemporary Russia which is suffering, the Russia of miracles, heroic deeds, martyrdom. This communion is possible if we establish here also the same intense religious life, creating here in exile an extension of our fatherland. This will perhaps draw older people away from their political dissensions, and will bring the young nearer to the Church by showing them the true meaning of Russia.

†

From the thirty-sixth chapter of Ecclesiasticus we can construct a beautiful prayer for Russia. Here are some excerpts: 'Have mercy upon us, O Lord the God of all, and behold . . . Show new signs and work divers wonders . . . Hasten the time . . . and let them declare Thy mighty works . . . Have compassion upon the city of Thy sanctuary, Jerusalem . . . and raise up the prophecies that have been in Thy name.' (Ecclesiasticus xxxvi. 1, 6, 8, 13, 15.)

†

How far astray we are led by false ideals! In this way many revolutionaries have lost their souls: starting from a correct (but narrow) concept of the good of the people, they have ended up with nothing but satanic hatred, falsehood, murder. A similar fate awaits the adherents of the ideal of nationalism unless they subordinate this ideal to the highest ideal of all.

†

Our whole interior life is set in motion by the love of God. But whence can we acquire this love? All our loves are fed by concrete impressions of the beloved object (the world, our friends and loved ones). How shall our love and faith be kept alive and not wither, if they are not nourished by outward evidence? Yet what concrete impression can we receive of God, whom 'no man hath seen at any time' (John i. 18)? We have Christ. Meditation on Him, prayer, the reading of the Gospels—such is the food by which the love of Christ is nourished. But it may be (and such is often the case) that our hearts are too coarse, too unreceptive. In that case, we must turn to the Lives of the Saints, to the writings of the

40

Fathers. They hold the same light of Christ, but with a softer quality, subdued by passing through the prism of a saintly, but purely human, soul.

†

It is better to live in such a way that we start with our own personal experience and pass from this to certain general ideas, rather than proceeding *vice versa*. Otherwise, we shall only be making verbal judgements about the experience of others, without having experienced these things ourselves: but unfortunately this is precisely what we usually do in spiritual questions.

†

Even if we adopt the viewpoint of the most violent atheism, the standpoint of believers is still safer and firmer than that of atheism: the latter is sheer bankruptcy. For is it not better to possess hopes and promises, rather than to be deprived of these as well as everything else?

†

Vespers, especially if I do not officiate myself, I find definitely difficult and even boring. I also feel boredom on behalf of those who 'attend the service'; it seems to me that they may well be 'attending' but that they pray badly. I would like to feel closer to them, I long for a really corporate prayer, for the doing away of those square yards of shining floor between us, for an end to our mutual estrangement. On the other hand, how easy to celebrate a *Moleben* or *Panikhida*[1] for the intentions of people whom I know

---

[1] *Moleben*: a short service of thanksgiving or intercession, usually held for a particular person or family.

Panikhida: a memorial service for the departed.

The priest officiates at these services in front of a small table set in the body

well or of those in whom I sense good, prayerful souls, as they stand close to me and enter into the meaning of the prayers. But why is it easy for me to pray when I am active and far more difficult to participate silently in other people's prayer? Is this not vanity, a kind of fluorescence or borrowed radiance kindled under the influence of other people's rays?

†

Nearly always, while attending church, I feel how very much we need to have family prayers and to practise other Church observances at home. What I have read in this connection about the normal custom in England confirms my conviction of such a necessity. We need to read the Bible, especially the Gospels, together with the Lives of the Saints and works of the Church Fathers; also our modern theologians such as Father Paul Florensky and Bulgakov. Today I read to my wife passages from the Fathers and the Epistle to the Corinthians–she is very eager. I wish we could make it a firm habit. Even after this brief experience I sense an opening, feel peculiarly elated. Tomorrow–a story from the Fioretti.[1]

†

For those who do not accept any exterior forms of religion: these are just as necessary to us, as saving, as intimately linked to religion, as the body is to the soul.

†

---

of the church, with the people standing round him. At Vespers, on the other hand, he is most of the time in the sactuary behind the iconostasis (icon screen), and so is comparatively distant from the congregation.

[1] Note written before ordination.

Only men who have no experience in such things can speak of the uselessness of making an effort in prayer or in the love of God. All striving towards God—however weak or forced—yields a vivid and irrefutable experience of His love. Anyone who has had this experience will never forget it. The same can be said of love towards other men. All love carries with it its own satisfaction and reward. Here we find the empirical verification of the words 'God is Love'.

†

The indifference of believers is something far more dreadful than the fact that unbelievers exist.

†

The new Orthodox conception of the Devil is that of a non-entity, of a shadow. The majestic figure of Mephistopheles is alien to us. The Devil is not loftiness—he is mediocrity and triviality.

†

The practice of theosophy, occultism, spiritualism is not only harmful in its effect on the health of the mind, but has as its basis an illegitimate desire to peer through a closed door. We must humbly admit the existence of a Mystery, and not try to slip round by the backstairs to eavesdrop. Moreover, we have been given a supreme law of life which leads us straight to God—love, a difficult, thorny path; but we must follow it, bearing our cross, with no excursions into byways.

†

The death of our friends and relations provides empirical confirmation of our faith in the infinite. Our love for the departed is an affirmation of the existence of another world. In the company of the dying, we reach the frontier dividing two worlds—the world of illusions and the real world: death proves to us the reality of what we held to be an illusion, and the insubstantiality of what we considered real.

†

The man who denies his relationship with God, who refuses to be His son, is not a real man but a man stunted, the unfinished plan of a man. For to be sons of God is not only granted us as a gift but is also *entrusted* to us as a task, and only the accomplishment of this task, through the conscious putting on of Christ and God, can lead to a full disclosure, a full blossoming, of each human personality.

†

Sin is a destructive force—and first of all it destroys the person burdened with it. Sin distorts and darkens the face of a man, even in the physical sense.

†

What is it that terrifies us most in ourselves? The state of insensibility, of spiritual sloth, blindness. What pain, what remorse should be occasioned by sin, what a thirst for contrition and forgiveness the soul should feel! But usually we experience nothing of the sort. And life goes on around us as if all were right with the world. Perhaps this indifference is the result precisely of the spiritual dissolution resulting from sin.

†

It often saddens us to see our dear ones looking faded and aged. Yet this decay of our person on the human and physical level opens the way for blessed spiritual forces which well up within us from the depths. The fading, the decline which we observe with dismay in ourselves and in others—the fading of bright eyes, of coloured cheeks, of deep melodious voices—all that is but the fading of our natural and corporeal nature and is of no value. The more the outer man decays, the more the inner man is reborn. It is well if this happens, provided the process of growing old does not lead instead to depression, to the fear of old age and death, to a spiritual deterioration.

†

The benefit of obedience: the soul frees itself for things interior when its exterior life is taken over by someone else, as in military service, the monastery, the family (obedience to husband, parents).

†

There is the monastic life and the state of marriage. The third condition, that of virginity in the world, is extremely dangerous, fraught with temptation, and beyond the strength of most people. Moreover, those who adhere to this condition are also a danger to the persons around them: the aura and beauty of virginity, which, when deprived of direct religious significance, are in a sense 'nuptial feathers', exercise a powerful attraction and awaken unedifying emotions.

†

Marriage is a revelation and a mystery. We see in it the complete transformation of a human being, the expansion of his personality, fresh vision, a new perception of life, and through it a rebirth into the world in a new plenitude.

Our modern individualism creates special difficulties in married

45

life. To overcome them, a conscious effort on both sides is neces-sary, in order to build up the marriage and make it a 'walking in the presence of God'. (The Church alone provides a full and genuine solution for all problems.) And there is something further, something which may appear to be the simplest thing of all, but which is nevertheless the most difficult to achieve—a firm intention to allow each partner to preserve his or her proper place in the marriage—for the wife humbly to assume the second place, for the husband to take up the burden and the responsibility of being the head. If this firm intention and desire are present, God will always help us to follow this difficult path, the path of martyrdom—the chant of the 'Holy martyrs' is sung in the course of the bridal procession—but also a way of life that yields the most intense joy.

†

Marriage, fleshly love, is a very great sacrament and mystery. Through it is accomplished the most real and at the same time the most mysterious of all possible forms of human relationship. And, qualitatively, marriage enables us to pass beyond all the normal rules of human relationship and to enter a region of the miraculous, the superhuman.

†

In fleshly love, besides its intrinsic value as such, God has granted the world a share in His omnipotence: man creates man, a new soul is brought into being.

†

Man enters deeply into the texture of the world through his family alone.

†

Neither the man, nor (still less) the woman, possesses absolute power over the other partner in the marriage. Coercion exercised over the will of another—even in the name of love—kills love itself. And so the question arises: must one submit to coercion if it threatens that which is most precious? A countless number of unhappy marriages result from precisely this—that each partner considers him or herself as the owner of the loved one. This is the cause of nearly all the difficulties of married life. The highest wisdom in marriage is shown by giving full freedom to the person you love: for our human marriage is the counterpart of the marriage in heaven between Christ and the Church, where there is absolute freedom.

†

Woman has been called the 'weaker vessel'. This 'weakness' consists especially in her enslavement to the natural, elemental forces within and outside herself. The result is inadequate self-control, irresponsibility, passionateness, blindness in judgement. Scarcely any woman is free from all these defects; she is always the slave of her passions, of her dislikes, of her desires. In Christianity alone does woman become man's equal, submitting her temperament to higher principles, and so acquiring moderation, patience, the ability to think rationally, wisdom. Only then does friendship with the husband become possible.

†

'The kingdom of God cometh not with observation . . . for behold, the kingdom of God is within you' (Luke xvii. 20–21). Could not the same be said of the eternal fire? Is not hell already here for many people?

†

47

We must not live 'lightly', but with the greatest possible tension of all our forces, both physical and spiritual. When we expend the maximum of our powers, we do not exhaust ourselves but increase the sources of our strength.

†

The woman who has 'a spirit of infirmity', so Christ affirmed, had been 'bound by Satan' (Luke xiii. 11, 16). Here we are shown another source of sickness—the devil. This is an objection which can be raised against those—for instance, myself—who declare that one must rejoice in sickness, as in all other misfortunes, and not ask to be healed.

†

We see the world not as it is in reality but as our imagination and will would have it be. And each of us sees it differently, in his own way, often placing insignificant objects in the foreground and leaving no place whatever for the only things that are really important.

†

I see a secret fear of death in the way men seek to escape loneliness.

†

I am reading Isaac the Syrian,[1] and I find him very close to my heart. I wanted to read him for a long time, but I thought that such reading was for the most perfect only. It seems, however, that

---

[1] Nestorian bishop of Nineveh towards the end of the seventh century, author of many mystical treatises written in Syriac.

he also offers much wise advice to beginners—such as we shall probably remain up to our death.

†

It is absolutely impossible to convince anyone of the existence of God, for all that can be said in words concerning faith can in no way convey the essential point about it, which is something altogether inexpressible. The arguments in favour of belief are not against reason, but beyond it. It is only in the light of love that reason accepts the apparent absurdities of faith.

†

Why is faith difficult? Before the fall man *knew*. Sin has hidden God from him, and faith is the piercing through this veil of sin which separates us from God.

Purification from sin leads from faith to knowledge.

†

The lust for riches may appear a sin of secondary importance, but in reality it is an extraordinarily important one—in fact, it is at the same time a real denial of faith in God and of love for mankind, and a partiality for baser things. It breeds malice, hardness of heart, continual anxiety. Its defeat is a partial victory over all these different kinds of sin.

†

Wherein lies the allurement and the poison of the theatre—for the spectator, and especially for the actor? The habit of living, and living intensely and keenly at that, an illusory life which is frequently far more vivid than our real, everyday existence; the

49

fact of creating in ourselves 'parasitical' personalities (from that of Yepikhodov to that of Tsar Fedor Ioannovich in the case of Moskvin);[1] vainglory. That is why the theatre is so dangerous for people of weak character; it grinds them in pieces until nothing is left. But then, all human activity contains these (or other) poisons, and it is only strong characters that are not overcome by them, but succeed in remaining themselves.

†

Blindness toward our own sins is due to partiality. Probably we *see* many things, but we *estimate* them wrongly, we make excuses for them and relate them incorrectly to each other—this is an almost instinctive reaction. It is most important for our salvation 'to see our own sins'. To love the Truth more than ourselves, to reject self—this is the beginning of salvation.

†

The attention which religion recommends us to give to our inner life is no less fruitful from the purely psychological viewpoint: it enables us to develop the power of attention, to concentrate our conscious life, and reveals new psychic powers.

If we peruse the writings of the saints and Fathers of the Church, what depths of psychological analysis we discover in them, what fine distinctions between different states of the soul, what great precision in defining and classifying all our varying sensations!

†

One of the Fathers—I do not remember which—draws an

---

[1] The roles of Yepikhodov (in Chekhov's *Cherry Orchard*) and of Tsar Fedor (in the tragedy by Alexis Tolstoy) were the most popular in the repertoire of Moskvin, the celebrated actor of the Moscow Arts' Theatre.

analogy between attention during prayer and the wick of an oil lamp. To develop this analogy further, the 'holy oil' of prayer, the express condition of the lamp's burning, is a continual state of contrition, of humility, purity of heart, and absence of anger.

†

Typical of the errors which lead to censoriousness, to depression, to wrong evaluations, is 'Rousseauism' in religion—the idea that here on earth, before the Last Judgement and condemnation, there can be flawless achievements on our part, and on the part of other men, in our human relationships.

Consequently we expect of ourselves the perfection of sanctity and are disheartened when, in our holiest moments, we discover in our hearts impurity, vainglory, duplicity; we are irritated when men we had considered flawless prove to be cowardly, malicious, untruthful; we despair when we see in God's own Church schisms, disputes, jealousies, envy—the unleashed storm of human passions.

And yet 'such things must needs be' (Mark xiii. 7); the entire world is infected with sin; the terrible fissure runs through it from top to bottom—the corruption of decay and death—and no one and nothing can be free of it. If, in the most perfect of all communities, among Christ's disciples, there was a Judas, why be shocked by a Vvedensky[1] in the Russian Church? Every parish has its lesser Judas, but it also has its meek, 'spirit-bearing' John, its faithful, active Peter.

†

---

1 Alexander Vvedensky (1889–1946), Russian priest, leader of the so-called 'Living Church', a schismatic movement which in 1922 broke away from the true Russian Orthodox Church under Patriarch Tikhon. Vvedensky's movement, which collaborated with the Communists, enjoyed spectacular successes at first, but soon ceased to be of any importance.

The joy afforded by the veneration of icons is caused by the fact that God, 'the Word Incomprehensible', came down from heaven, was made flesh, took human form, and dwelt among us, 'full of grace and truth', so that we have heard Him with our ears, seen Him with our eyes, touched Him with our hands (1 John i. 1).

The basic feature of our religious life is an eager striving to apprehend the holy in concrete, palpable form; we love to touch it, to kiss it, to wear it on our breast, to bless our houses with it. The Iconoclasts[1] tried to deprive us of these sacred objects, and when they were restored there was great joy in The Church. See how cold and abstract the faith is in denominations which reject the veneration of icons! While openly rejecting the icons, they unconsciously deny the Incarnation. How degenerate their Christianity becomes; and the Eucharist itself, which is the focus of Christian life, becomes disembodied and loses its significance. Indeed, if among us the Word has become flesh, among them the Flesh has become word; they reduce the divine Flesh, communion in which gives life eternal (John vi. 51) to mere words and reasoning.

†

Types of Christianity: (1) intellectual-contemplative; (2) volitional and active (Catholicism); (3) intellectual-ethical (Protestantism); and (4) Christianity understood as supreme Beauty—Orthodoxy. All the powers of the faithful are given up to this vision. All other aspects of Christianity are subordinated to this conception. Some people—the Old Believers[2]—think that Orthodoxy is concerned exclusively with liturgical worship: there is some truth in this—Orthodoxy is to live theurgically, 'without

---

[1] Iconoclasts ('icon-smashers'): a movement in the Christian east during the eighth and ninth centuries, which objected to any form of representational art in church decoration. The Iconoclasts were condemned by the seventh Ecumenical Council (A.D. 787).

[2] See p. 14, n. 2.

leaving the Temple'. But at the same time this attitude presents certain dangers—as soon as this ideal grows dim a man is left without a trained will, without moral and intellectual discipline. That is why the disintegration of Orthodoxy—in contemporary Russia, for example—leads to dissoluteness, immorality, ignorance. The human element is not sufficiently cultivated in the Orthodox—especially in members of the Old Believer sect—and so, when deprived of faith, they became a slave of the world. And yet we reject all inferior types of Christianity, whether rational, volitional, or ethical. But we need to discipline our religious will-power, raise our cultural and moral level, and become worthy of the precious gift entrusted to us.

†

For many, Orthodoxy is merely a 'world-outlook'.

†

I realize more and more clearly that Orthodoxy is the principle of absolute freedom. It entails a fear of rules and regulations, a fear of limiting ourselves in one way or another, of placing the word, the thought, the ornamentation above the fact or outside the fact; an aversion to propaganda and constraint—even of a purely ideological or psychological kind—a fear of indoctrination. It means putting our whole faith in the actual presence of religious life—all the rest will come of itself.

†

The mistake of our cultured classes at the beginning of the century was to approach Christianity by-passing the Church, by-passing theology and philosophy. Their approach was aesthetic, emotional, and social, or else pure routine. The peculiarity and essence of the new Orthodox theology lies in its distinctive attitude towards antiquity and the Old Testament. As such it is not 'literary', but represents a genuine living experience vitally connected with the Church.

†

A feature of the Russian Orthodox faith which is essential, yet hidden from many—a feature connected neither with the exterior organization of the Church nor with its dogmatic and liturgical peculiarities, but with the life of the Russian people on the deepest and most fundamental level. Beneath the external divisions into geographical units (dioceses, parishes), there exists another organization of living elements in the Orthodox Church, which does not coincide with the first and is constructed on other, non-territorial principles. Its centres are a few personalities, highly gifted spiritually. The field of action of these *startsy* is unlimited, they come to assume their role through free election, through the voluntary submission of others to their guidance. Although not yet canonized by the Church, they are undoubtedly saints, recognized as such by the people.

I feel that in our tragic days it is precisely through this means that faith will survive and be strengthened in our country.

†

One of the features which distinguishes our theology from that of the Catholics: it does not look at things legalistically, but in terms of God's grace.

†

Concerning the doubts aroused by the words of X: 'In their relations with the workers, the members of Catholic Youth Circles at the beginning not only avoid calling themselves Catholics but do not even mention Christ.' This is to go down to their level in order to bring them up to our level—to start by establishing brotherly confidence and sympathy, and then to embark on explanations. 'Let us love one another, that with one accord we may confess. . . .'[1] Are there steps and degrees of initiation? If there are, then all is clear. 'The milk of the word', in St. Peter's phrase (1 Peter ii. 2). 'Unto the Jews I became as a Jew' (1 Cor. ix. 20).

†

Attitude toward adherents to other faiths:
Respect their faith.
Show an interest, ask questions, speak to them about our faith.
Invite them to our church services.
Do not be embarrassed about explaining our faith.
Pray for them.

†

. . . Several days have elapsed, and I can hardly recall—and even so not from within but only in an exterior fashion—that extraordinary feeling which came over me as we laid N. in her coffin.

It is always the most dreadful, and even hideous, moment: the undertakers, to whom all this fuss over the dead is nothing but a routine duty, drag the body from the bed; it hangs helplessly, the head dangling—and they shove it into the coffin. The members of the family are usually sent out of the room—and so much the better.

But this time, it was altogether different: there were no strangers; the priest, holding a lighted candle, prayed in silence and the members of the family lifted the dead woman and lowered her gently into the coffin.

---

[1] Words sung by the deacon during the Holy Liturgy, shortly before the recitation of the Creed.

For a few seconds I had a most extraordinary feeling: I literally stepped out of myself, so that I seemed to be not just an onlooker but a participant; it seemed that everything was exactly as it should be, that the scene was like a painting on an icon, and that I was part of it. I am now afraid to describe it wrongly: it was somehow like a holy vision of the world. Thus do children and saints conceive the church and the divine service, as something taking place at the same time in two worlds (a boy's words: 'It is as if God embraced the whole church and held it in His hands').

On a lower level it is an aesthetic perception of the world, which one sees transfigured in a heavenly way.

†

The certainty that all the prophecies have been accomplished, that the times are fulfilled, and that humanity is close to the final consummation which will issue in terrible catastrophe for some and immeasurable joy for others—such a certainty, it seems, is an inevitable experience in all intense religious life. It is a sudden awareness and realization of infinity—an experience inherent, perhaps, in all strong feeling—be it despair, love, an impulse of faith, or prophetic ecstasy.

†

Birth is mystical—we are visited by a messenger from another world. This mystic sense is even more deeply awakened in us by the death of those we love—when they leave us, they draw a long cable from the tissues of our soul, so that we can no longer be content to live in this world alone; a telephone communicating with the infinite is thus installed in our warm, comfortable home.

†

I always feel sad about the slow ebb of spiritual life after Easter. First, there is an increase in spiritual forces as we enter deeper into Lent. Everything inward becomes considerably easier; our soul is purer and more at peace; our love is greater and our prayer better. Then come the days of Holy Week which are always so remarkable; and after that the joy of Easter. I do not know how to thank God for letting me participate in all this so fully as a priest. But then comes Saturday of Easter week, the doors into the sanctuary are closed as if the gates of heaven had been locked,[1] and everything becomes more difficult, the soul grows weaker, becomes faint-hearted and lazy, every spiritual effort is hard.

†

I feel so deeply the breath of the devil in self-love, which devours souls, destroys families, ruins all social work. For the Christian it should be sufficient to remember the Apostle's words: 'Why do ye not rather suffer wrong?' (1 Cor. vi. 7). But the cunning human mind immediately discovers a loop-hole, namely, that one is not angry on one's own behalf but on behalf of justice and so forth. Generally speaking, how great are the difficulties God meets in men, how stubbornly they build up hell, how little they desire light and blessedness! The longer one lives, the more certain one is of Satan's power. . . .

†

He who follows the good impulse of his heart, enriches above all else his own self: a radiant, healing force enters his soul, a joy

---

[1] This refers to the gates of the iconostasis (the screen of icons separating the sanctuary from the body of the church). Outside service time these gates are as a rule always closed, and they are also kept closed at many points during the services themselves. In the week after Easter, alike during and outside services, the gates are kept constantly open.

and peace which cure all the ailments and ulcers of our soul. On the other hand, the man who hardens himself constricts his heart and lets in the cold, enmity, death.

†

Our lack of compassion, hardness of heart, and mercilessness towards others form an impenetrable curtain between ourselves and God. It is as if we had covered a plant with a black hood, and then complained because it died from lack of sunlight.

†

Evil is not just a bad habit, an incorrect attitude of the soul— it is in reality something inspired by the power of the devil. This is especially obvious in the feeling of anger.

†

'Lay not up for yourselves treasures upon earth . . . take no thought' (Matt. vi. 19, 34). Why?

Earthly riches are corruptible.

They are useless—'the life of man does not depend on the wealth of his estate.'

They require care and worry and are therefore harmful even from the worldly point of view.

They enslave our heart: 'Where your treasure is, there will your heart be also' (Matt. vi. 21).

Care and anxiety about them are godless, for they presuppose the absence of Providence: compare the parable of the rich man (Luke xii. 16–21).

They weaken our spiritual powers: 'Take heed to yourselves, lest at any time your hearts be overcharged with surfeiting, and drunkenness, and cares of this life . . .' (Luke xxi. 34).

They make us put things the wrong way round: 'Seek ye first the kingdom of God, and His righteousness' (Matt. vi. 33).
They determine our destiny on earth and after death.

†

'The works of the flesh are manifest, which are these: . . . idolatry, witchcraft, hatred, variance, emulations, wrath, strife, seditions, heresies . . .' (Gal. v. 19–20). What has the flesh to do with these sins? They result from a special condition of the body, from languor, tension, the turmoil of the blood. The law of James Lange[1] explains many things. Note also the immense importance of bodily processes in all the movements of our soul— whether in sin or in prayer.

†

'*Mania grandiosa*' (megalomania) inevitably arises from our being wrapped up in ourselves. All sense of proportion is lost, and the ego develops and grows till it reaches the domain of madness.

†

For wisdom's sake we must prepare our soul to accept the 'engrafted word' (James 1. 21)—in silence, meekness, concentration and purity.
Here are the opposites: an unbridled tongue (instead of silence and listening); a loose emotionalism, quick to sin; impurity, anger, shallowness, forgetfulness.

†

---

[1] Compare p. 123.

59

Being creatures of psyche and flesh, with the spiritual element within us but feebly developed, we cannot fully apprehend God and therefore we often deny His existence. We are like blind men, who deny the existence of the light just because they cannot see it.

†

'Depart from me, for I am a sinful man, O Lord!' (Luke v. 8). This story from the Gospel contains, like every Gospel story, however short, many lessons: (1) a lesson of obedience: we must do as we are told, even though it goes against common sense; (2) life according to one's own will and to the will of God—how different are the results! (3) fear in the face of the manifestation of God's grace.

It is wrong to think that Christ took pity on all and forgave everybody. He was at times severe and awe-inspiring, and the approach of light was terrifying for falsehood and sin. The fear of God is the beginning of wisdom, the beginning of repentance, the beginning of salvation. 'I am a sinful man': such is the cry of repentance.

†

'Nervousness' is in a certain sense the psycho-somatic condition of holiness. A body that has been refined and transformed by tears, fasting, sickness, and toil, becomes more susceptible to the influence of beneficent spiritual forces. But at the same time it grows morbidly sensitive to the world of gross material objects, and its reaction towards this world takes the form of nervousness.

A saint, minus his saintliness, is a neurotic. (Striking words of a doctor who visited Mount Athos:[1] 'They are all neurasthenics in there.')

---

[1] A peninsula in northern Greece, entirely devoted to monastic settlements: since the tenth century, the chief centre of Orthodox monasticism.

A saint who has fallen and lost his sanctity becomes an easy prey to demons; that is why the Fathers of the Church assert that the state of one who has relapsed from a high standard of spiritual discipline is more dangerous than that of a person who is entirely unreligious. Herein lies the danger of fasting and asceticism, when not regulated by an experienced director and when emptied of the content of prayer.

†

Black 'grace'. An influx of extraordinary powers, an almost unlimited expansion of energy, can be observed in people during a fit of anger. If it is true that 'when a man is kind, none can withstand him', it is also true that when a man is angry, it is no less difficult to withstand his strength. A man who abandons himself to irritable moods, has opened his soul to demonic forces.

†

A feature common to all the devil's temptations—the temptations of bread, miracle-working, power (Matt. iv. 1–11); of the flesh, the soul, and the spirit—is the fact that they are subtle, not gross: in his temptations he does not use ordinary human means of seduction. There is no recourse to obvious, gross sins. But all three temptations involve a rejection of freedom, that is, of faith and love for Truth. Sins of sensuality, vanity, and love of power are only suggested indirectly. These sins recur in history, in the form of socialism, occultism, and *étatisme* (idolatry of the state).

†

Why did saints, before attaining sanctity, so often possess quite mediocre gifts, if one may say so? Perhaps because our outstanding but carnal gifts interfere with the development of the gifts of grace.

For example, let us take memory. A person may have a weak human memory and yet, at a moment of inspiration, remember all that is necessary. I often experience this during confession, addresses, or sermons: necessary quotations and examples, precise words, come to me spontaneously. This is why, perhaps, taking notes, and other trivial methods of memorizing, are a sign of lack of faith in God's power—'my strength is made perfect in weakness . . . for when I am weak, then am I strong' (2 Cor. xii. 9–10). But something else is also true: everything requires labour, effort.

†

In the text '. . . let him take up his cross, and follow me' (Luke ix. 23), in the Latin there is a word omitted in the Russian translation—*quotidie* (daily): *et tollat crucem suam quotidie et sequatur me.*

The thought of bearing one's cross daily.

†

There are men of a wonderful, paradisiac character, with souls born before Adam's fall—childlike in their simplicity and direct, knowing nothing of anger and untruth. And this is not the result of a struggle within themselves, of an effort; they are born that way—without sin. And, curiously enough, it constantly happens that these men stand outside the Church, and sometimes live entirely without religion. They are too simple, too much of a piece to engage in theological speculation, and also too modest and shy to express their feelings in words or signs (i.e. rites). In religion the most important thing is not faith but the love of God, and they love God because they love Beauty, Goodness, and Truth—all of which are elements of Divinity. How many claim to be believers, and yet lack this sense of Beauty and Goodness:

there are sin and anger in their souls and they are entirely indifferent to Truth—for them, its place is taken by a dozen or so little truths to which they cling proudly. But these others—the true and simple souls who live in joy even on earth—will, I feel sure, enter after death into the kingdom of Light and Joy. By the attraction of affinity, they are in their native element when in the company of saints—of simple and blessed souls. We, the so-called 'believers', say 'I will go' (Matt. xxi. 30), and do not move: they make no statement, but simply fulfil the Father's will.

†

X's genius rests on two qualities: his sincerity, his ability to look at the world without distortion and prejudice, with a fresh vision; and his taste for things. He *loves* the world, no matter whether it is a new book, an olive tree, or an encounter with another person.

†

What do you think of immortality? An imaginary question put to X (who is very close to being a just man). He would answer, quite correctly: 'I do not think about it at all'.

Perhaps the commandments to 'become as little children' (Matt. xviii. 3) and to 'take no thought for the morrow' (Matt. vi. 34) contain also another piece of advice: to trust God in this question, too.

†

True love regards as infidelity and as a sin against the beloved all delight, any strong response, which has been experienced separately, as well as all association with other people—even the partaking of food prepared by strange hands.

In love thère is a real, actual merging into one; hence the pain caused by all separation, by the fact of not being one.

†

The transcendent aspect of the relationship between husband and wife is the true essence of matrimony.

†

Youthful entanglements and complexes—Hamletism—usually spring from the following sources: take a talented young man (more rarely, a girl) endowed with intelligence, imagination, a vividly impressionable nature. Under the influence of books, examples, persons, and with the aid of that very intelligence and imagination, he creates parallel personalities in himself, a whole wardrobe of masks and costumes. These are like larvae—they stifle the original kernel of personality and multiply, covering it with a parasitic growth. Hence complexity, entanglements, inevitable falsifications and loss of personality. Only through strenuous effort will the true personality rediscover itself among all these parasites and find its way through this noisy, motley crowd. One may destroy these parasites by despising and ignoring them and by limiting the sphere of one's interests. But it is almost impossible to achieve this without the aid of a friend or a priest, for real personality can be so stifled and suppressed that its rediscovery offers the greatest difficulties; the inexperienced prefer the risk of giving new strength to their own larvae. The usual result of this is a muddled life, a wrongly chosen profession; in the worst cases, insanity.

†

Broken, faulty speech, with pauses and searchings for words, is often the characteristic of a very sincere person, who is unable to use *clichés*, and gropes painfully for his own words and for exact expressions. That is why I am always sympathetic towards a certain kind of tongue-tied speech—provided, of course, that it is not a sign of sheer incapacity.

†

How shall we answer the usual demand of the unbelievers, that 'proof' should be given immediately, right on the spot? You do not try to demonstrate a scientific, mathematical truth to a drunkard. The same can be said here: first sober yourself of your intoxication with the world—its bustle, worries, vanity—and then we shall enter into conversation, and you will be able to understand. 'Wisdom will not enter into a soul that deviseth evil' (Wisdom i. 4).

†

The common feeling that our world is the only one, is founded on a complete unbelief in the 'kingdom of heaven'. The sorrow felt for the departed is lack of faith, paganism. We must acquire the Christian consciousness of the reality of the kingdom of heaven.

†

Self-denial, which is so often mentioned in connection with the practice of Christianity, is conceived by some as an end in itself; they look upon it as the essential point of every Christian's life.

But it is only a *way* and a *means* for achieving our end—the putting on of Christ.

Neither must we think, as others do—going to the opposite extreme—that self-denial means renouncing one's personality, one's own path, a sort of spiritual suicide. Quite the contrary: self-denial is liberation from the slavery of sin (without self-denial we are prisoners), and the free manifestation of our true essence as originally designed for us by God.

†

Love is love only when it is addressed to all without exception. As long as it is directed only towards those whom 'I' love, it is nothing but selfishness. I speak of Christian love, not love in marriage or the family.

†

The sight of death is always edifying. However it occurs, it is always a miracle and a mystery. Our thoughts and—if the dead person is dear to us—our love seem to cross the threshold together with the dying, so that we receive a glimpse into another world and are convinced of its reality. I experienced this for the first time when I saw someone tread on an earwig and 'bring it to naught'. Then I realized for the first time that nothing can be destroyed, that this would be nonsense which neither our mind nor our spirit could bear, that even the earwig had passed into another world: it had vanished, indeed, from the realm of being as we know it, but had not been destroyed.

†

To define and formulate one's pain sometimes means to be freed from it (that is why reflective people possess a feeble sensitivity).

†

Modern civilization was produced by a creative effort of humanity, not only independent of, but often contrary to, the law of God. It acquired solid, robust, anti-religious forms, invested with an alien spirit which is hostile to us.

How shall we solve this problem, we who want to live in

accordance with God's law, yet do not wish to leave the world? It is easier to take a decision as an individual—to go into the world without losing ourselves, keeping our heart dedicated to Christ, to live to the full the life of the Church, without being over-indulgent towards ourselves.

For society this solution is much more difficult.

Catholicism provides us with an example of an energetic 'muz-zling' of the world: the world is forced to live in accordance with the Church, to be the Church's servant.

But I do not think that this problem can be solved by individual forces, not even by those of the Church. We cannot pass through the world unarmed; this would only be false pride. We must use the weapons of this world. We must humbly admit statesmanship, the external methods of exercising influence upon the world. The fact that we have lost Russia is not only a political mistake, but a sin against the Church.[1]

†

In our emigration the view is sometimes expressed that con-temporary Russia is all darkness, blood, mud, and that a spark of the truth has been saved only by the emigration. This is the psy-chology of the Varangians waiting to be called back and to light a flame in the darkness.[2] As long as such a mood exists among us, we dare not return to our Mother Country where men are answer-able with their own blood for their faith and for all the things that we here enjoy freely, which we 'talk' about but hardly live by.

†

---

[1] Unfinished.

[2] According to the medieval Russian Primary Chronicle, the Varangians (or Vikings) who levied tribute over the Eastern Slavs were expelled by the latter and later—in the ninth century—were invited to return and establish order in Russia.

67

The celebration of this great day[1] has been marked but feebly, due to the extreme weakness of our faith. The central administration should have given instructions for the organization of a special week of prayer and recollection,[2] with frequent sermons to instruct the faithful. But today, at the Liturgy, when I said: 'With fear of God and with faith draw near',[3] nobody came up. This entire year should have been proclaimed a special year of fasting and prayer, of a great purification of the Church.

In this we might well learn from the Catholics—how they keep their flock in hand, how skilfully they educate them.

†

When the times are fulfilled and the end is at hand, when the world's autumn comes and God sends his angels to reap the harvest —what will they find in the barren fields of our hearts? And yet, the time is nearly accomplished and the end close by for each of us, the end which we shall each face even before the common harvest.

But let us not be downhearted. See how the sower goes on sowing among the rocks and thorns and by the roadside. This means that he places some hope even in such fields as these. And we know from the lives of the saints how often a soul which had seemed irreclaimably stifled by sin, blinded by passion, hardened

---

[1] 2/15 January 1933, the hundredth anniversary of the death of St. Seraphim of Sarov (1759–1833), one of the most celebrated and best loved of all the Russian saints.

[2] 'Prayer and recollection': in Russian, *govenie*. A *govenie* in some respects corresponds to the western practice of 'going into retreat'. It is a special period of prayer and fasting (lasting perhaps a week) with frequent attendance at Church services, undertaken usually as a preparation for confession and communion.

[3] Words in the Liturgy, said by the priest just before the communion of the people, as he comes out of the sanctuary with the chalice.

in evil, became good ground, fertile and productive, purified of poisonous mixtures and alien seeds.

†

The essence of faith and religious life does not lie in a strained searching for proofs, but in effort and moral choice. Faith is a path leading to God, an experiment which is always successful. The righteous strove toward heaven and heaven received them. 'Draw nigh to God, and He will draw nigh to you' (James iv. 8).

†

Knowledge is gained through love.
Love of the world, of men, erotic love—these provide the best possibilities for acquiring knowledge.

†

We must not think that there is only one kind of wealth—money. One can be rich in youth, possess the assets of talent, of natural endowments, the capital of health. These riches, too, are obstacles to salvation.

Material wealth enslaves us, sharpening our self-interest, corroding our heart, overwhelming us with anxiety and fear; like an insatiable demon, it demands sacrifice. Instead of serving us, it usually makes us serve it. But is it not the same with the treasures of health, strength, youth, beauty, talent? Do not they likewise confirm us in our pride and imprison the heart, leading it away from God?

Yes, indeed: 'Blessed are the poor' in the world's goods. How easily they gain evangelical lightness of spirit and freedom from earthly fetters. But blessed also are those who lack health and youth, for 'he that hath suffered in the flesh hath ceased from sin'

(1 Peter iv. 1). Blessed are the ugly, the ungifted, the unsuccessful —they are free from the chief enemy, pride, for they have nothing to be proud of.

But what are we to do if God has granted us this or that earthly talent? Is it possible that we shall not be saved until we are divested of it? We may keep our riches (but not for ourselves) and still be saved; but we must be inwardly free of them; we must tear our heart away from them, and hold our treasures as if we did not hold them; possess them, but not let them possess us; lay them at Christ's feet and serve Him through them.

†

Our love of God is measured by our willingness to accept sufferings and misfortunes and to see in them the hand of God. We can find support in the fact that these sufferings are also the measure of the love that God bears us.

†

We often mistake for religion a vague mixture of the reminiscences of childhood, the sentimental emotions sometimes experienced in church, coloured eggs and cake at Easter. How shall we succeed in awakening in our soul any sense of the way of the cross which it must follow towards God? . . .[1]

†

It may be that we are angelically kind towards those who treat us with confidence and love. But once we encounter anger, criticism, hostility, this kindness is turned into its opposite. This clearly shows our complete helplessness in the face of evil, and—

---

[1] Unfinished.

first of all—in the face of the evil in ourselves, which rises up in us when provoked by the criticisms of others. Reproaches and criticism are a bitter medicine for our vanity, our self-satisfaction.

†

All pleasures and enjoyments degrade the soul, weakening it spiritually and undermining its strength. The meaning of suffering is this: it is a participation in the suffering of Christ, a building up of the body of Christ in the world (the Church), a bearing of the cross, a following of the example of the saints, incompatibility with the world.

†

The tension of effort, of work, always leads to the growth of our spiritual forces.

†

When we pray for the dead, we develop in ourselves a sense of the unreality of the present world—for a part of it which was dear to us is gone—and of the reality of that other world, whose actual existence is confirmed by our love for the dead.

†

. . . The older we grow the more we learn to appreciate the solidity of friendship in this precarious, untrustworthy, shadowy world. . . .

†

If we notice sin, it means that we participate in it—and precisely in that particular kind of sin. Does a child condemn debauchery?

He does not notice it. If we notice something, we share in it in some measure.

†

Sometimes it seems as if the souls of old people die gradually, along with their bodies. This impression that the soul is becoming impoverished is due to the fact that the body, as it grows senile, gradually ceases to be a sufficient medium of expression for the soul. The process is similar to what happens with transfers: the damp paper gives a faint outline of a picture (life); then this (the body) is gradually drawn away (sickness, old age). The picture disappears in parts, then fades entirely (death). All that remains in our hands is a blank sheet (the dead body), but if we look at the underside, we see a bright picture (the life of the world to come).

†

Plan of a work, which I have been thinking about for a long time: memory and the lack of it.

The meaning, moral and religious, of memory: its relation to gratitude and penitence.

I think that a feeble memory is one of the symptoms of a sinful condition. It contains the following sinful elements: incapacity for spiritual effort, absentmindedness, and insufficient love. Is a 'forgetful saint' conceivable? Of course not, because the saint has an active attitude towards everything, he extends to all things a concentrated attention and love. A feeble memory = a narrow consciousness. On the other hand, we must keep in view the positive value of a feeble memory, of forgetfulness; a partial loss of memory is often a direct advantage in the spiritual life. It frees us from what is wordly, from the burden of associations, reminiscences, knowledge, it makes it possible for us to be entirely direct— that is, sincere, inspired with genius; it makes it possible for us to live in the present moment, to be content with the act in which we are immediately engaged, with the person immediately before us—to be 'like children'; to perceive everything as if it were something new, to gaze upon the world with fresh eyes. Forgetfulness is the overcoming of time, the effacing of offences, the relief brought by obedience, the neglect of our own merits, the acquisition of simplicity. Memory, on the other hand, keeps everything in store, and only temporarily refuses to reproduce it. A forgetful old man resembles a passenger who has registered his luggage and waits, empty-handed, for the train. When the time comes, his suitcases will be opened by stern customs officials and he will be appalled by their contents.

†

'In the abundance of Thy glory Thou hast effaced Thine adversaries' (Exodus xv. 7)—such is the method of the spiritual struggle, the only possible method: to destroy, to 'efface' the enemy within us by the abundance and power of divine radiance.

†

Sin lies in *yielding* to evil thoughts, not in *having* them. We are never free from these thoughts, for such is our nature, obscured by sin; even the saints had evil thoughts. Our voluntary yielding to evil thoughts or our struggle against them—herein lies our defeat or our victory.

†

We are endowed with a purely Orthodox, ascetic feeling of 'sobriety' as opposed to 'spiritual intoxication', 'delight' and 'sweetness'. . . . This marks one of our differences with the Catholics. This difference is particularly evident in religious art.

†

Our life does not flow smoothly and regularly. It moves like every living process in the life of nature, being marked by moments of downfall and exaltation. Lent is a time of spiritual effort. If we cannot give God our entire life, let us at least devote the periods of fasting entirely to Him, let us make our prayer stronger, multiply our alms, control our passions, make peace with our enemies.

†

Nothing that God has created is evil; it is *we* who pervert, who turn into evil ourselves and all that surrounds us; this choice of evil depends on our free will.

†

No evil proceeds from God, who does not lead anyone astray. Each man brings temptation upon himself by his own sins. Sin generates not only sorrow but death as well.

†

'Tolstoyism' is the result of the laborious efforts of a mediocre intelligence to test all the foundations of human life, created by men of genius, by saints, by the spirit of great nations. And because that mediocre intelligence proves incapable of understanding the meaning of all these foundations, laws, and institutions, it is brought to deny them (Church, matrimony, religious rites, dress, etiquette, and so on). I have seen this clearly during my conversation with X (a Tolstoyan).

†

. . . There is perhaps a glimmer of hope in the fact that however weak we may be, however spiritually feeble and inclined to sin,

Christ still remains our sanctuary, immovable and ever desired, to which we shall always return.

†

We continually justify ourselves by saying, 'This is just a trivial sin', and we reassure ourselves: 'I will not allow myself to do anything worse'. But bitter experience has shown us all, many times, that once we have begun to give way to a sin, it takes possession of us: and then scarcely anyone has the strength to turn back.

†

It is characteristic that the two main types of insanity—megalomania and persecution mania—are possible only when encouraged by self-love. They are both forms of the sin of pride.

†

Living corpses walk in our midst. Their souls have died before their bodies, and they have no hope of resurrection; for it is *here* that we prepare for the life of the world to come. And there are souls which have already, as it were, risen from the dead before the death of the body: through their acts, experience, and love they have gained access to the highest levels of the spiritual life.

†

In this sombre world, even the radiance of each virtue casts its own shadow: humility—pusillanimity and cunning; kindness—injustice; the love of truth—over-exacting harshness. And since we are always inclined to see the worst, it is these shadows that we see first of all, and sometimes they are all we see. To our sinful gaze the meek appear lacking in strength and simplicity; those who are drawn to prayer seem arid and selfish; the generous and dis-interested seem impractical and extravagant; the contemplative seem lazy. The faculty of seeing the dark side of everything–even of good things–is not so much a proof that the darkness in fact exists where we imagine it to be: rather, it is clear evidence of darkness *in us*, of the sinfulness which we all share.

†

We must not only bear misfortunes but see in them the hand of the Master of destinies.

†

. . . I will tell you the conclusion that I have long since reached from reading the Holy Fathers: periods of aridity are entirely normal, and we must bear them patiently and with equanimity. These periods implant in us the humble realization of our helpless-ness and compel us to place in God alone all our hope for the revival of our hearts.

†

Life would become much easier for us, many things would fit into their right places, if we only thought more often about the ephemeral character of our life, about the ever-present possibility that we might die today. Then all the small miseries and trifles that preoccupy us would disappear of themselves, and things of greater meaning would occupy a more important place in our minds.

†

Life does not flow smoothly, and this 'unevenness' is a sort of general rule: our past prosperity is so far away (far away not outwardly only but also inwardly) that we do not even give it a sigh of regret. Of course, it is a commonplace, well known to all, and especially to us Russians, that suffering is good for the soul; but recently I have had a new experience of this tragic law. If we voluntarily take up the burden of our difficulties and sorrows—if we acquiesce in them—they fortify and feed our souls, they are transformed immediately into spiritual riches: 'For our light affliction, which is but for a moment, worketh for us a far more exceeding and eternal weight of glory' (2 Cor. iv. 17). It is a fair wind, filling the sails of our spirit. . . .

†

It is not righteousness in itself which is important, for the Pharisees too were righteous: but in their case it was a false righteousness, not based on what is essential—that is, on love and faith; it was an external righteousness, haughty, false, trebly unjust. All the virtues are nothing without humility.

What is the value of our righteousness, such as it is? Is it not combined with sin? Is it not formal and full of vanity?

†

The old lady X, who believes herself definitely secure from the religious point of view, when I bring her books to read: 'Ah, this is exactly what I think, I must copy this out.' A vain person is hopelessly blind and lonely; she sees nothing in the world or in other people except herself and what is hers.

†

Human limitations in themselves are not the same as stupidity.

77

The most intelligent people are inevitably limited in some respects. Stupidity begins with the appearance of obstinacy and self-assurance—that is, with the emergence of pride.

†

Good and evil are not just the sum total of good or evil deeds, but there is an evil or good force which possesses man. This pressure of evil, the force of this evil principle, is immeasurable. Acts in themselves have little religious significance. Those which are 'good' so far as their results are concerned—to give food and other assistance—can be basically bad if performed by a person who is possessed by evil; and actions which are ineffectual, foolish, or even harmful, can be good, if they come from a good source and are prompted by a good impulse.

†

Often we refrain from sin not because we have conquered it or overcome it inwardly, but thanks to outward circumstances: out of the sense of propriety, from the fear of punishment, and so on. But even a disposition towards sin is already in itself a sin.

However, an interior, latent sin is less serious than one which has been actually committed; in such a case we have not grown inveterate in sin, nor given temptation or caused harm to others. Often we feel a desire to sin, yet do not acquiesce but struggle against it.

The following are the stages through which sin enters into us: image, attention, interest, attraction, passion.

†

We do good deeds, purify our heart and draw nearer to God, not in order to obtain a reward but out of our love for God. One day I asked myself: would I remain with Christ if I knew for certain that the devil will defeat God? And I answered without hesitation: of course I would remain with Him. What has selfishness to do with it?

†

The inferiority-complex is nothing but pride, the concentration of attention on oneself, egoism under a different form. Neither megalomania nor a painful sense of one's own insignificance ever trouble the minds of the humble and simple.

†

Generally speaking, I am bored by the Canons,[1] and especially by the *Akathists*,[2] and I read them only out of a sense of duty. I make an exception only for the penitential Canons of the *Octoechos*[3] and the Lenten *Triodion*.[4] But there are times when my heart is very heavy and sad, and then I recite certain Canons—to the Mother of God and to the most Sweet Jesus—as if the words were my own. This means that our 'lack of feeling' for the Canons is an accusation against us—it points to an absence in the given person of the religious mood in which these Canons were written.

†

---

[1] Canon: a series of ecclesiastical hymns, arranged in nine 'Odes', and devoted usually to a particular theme—the Resurrection of Christ, the feast of a saint, repentance, or the like.

[2] *Akathist*: a set of twenty-four stanzas of religious poetry, devoted (like a Canon) to a particular subject. 'Akathist' (from the Greek *Akathistos*) means literally 'not sitting': all are supposed to stand while it is read or sung.

[3] *Octoechos*: the 'Book of the Eight Tones', one of the service books used in Orthodox worship.

[4] *Triodion*: the 'Book of the Three Odes', another service book, used in Lent.

Morality is not exactly a secondary matter in Christianity, but it is a *derivative* one. Our morality should issue naturally from the plenitude of our religion; if it does not, it is either mere respectability or a matter of instinct, or else—very often—an insufferable hypocrisy.

†

The more a man gives up his heart to God, to his vocation and to men, forgetful of himself and of that which belongs to him, the more lighthearted he will feel, until he attains peace, quiet, joy—the attributes of a simple and humble soul.

†

The First Epistle of St. John the Evangelist speaks of divine love, of that love which covers a multitude of sins, which cancels the Law and takes the place of all the commandments: that love which gives life because it brings us into contact with the Source of Life; which confers the highest knowledge: 'He that loveth not, knoweth not God' (1 John iv. 8), and, on the contrary, 'Every one that loveth . . . knoweth God' (1 John iv. 7)—knows God by the law of similarity.

We must think of ourselves as participating in this love, for each of us loves something, someone. Even if there are a few people who love nothing, who live here already in the 'darkness below', such cases are very rare. We all love our relatives, our family, our friends, the people who share our way of thinking. But is that the love which Christ expects from us? In regard to the love of family, it is clear to all that this is nothing but a selfish love, a love of that which is ours, of ourselves. And love of our relatives, of our friends, is it not also selfish? Among an endless number of things and persons we choose those whom we find congenial, enclose them within the enlarged bound sof our ego, and love them. But suffice that they forfeit something of the qualities which made us choose them, then we pour out on them the full measure of our hatred, contempt, and, at best, indifference. This kind of love is a human, natural, physical feeling, at times very valuable in this world, but it loses its meaning in the light of eternal life. It is precarious and easily turns into its opposite, acquiring a demoniac character.

If the spirit of love truly lived in us, we should embrace everyone in our love—good or evil, attractive or repulsive.

But how is this possible? The commandment of the Gospel cannot be impossible to fulfil; otherwise the Gospel would be a collection of beautiful sayings, inapplicable to real life. Equally inapplicable, so it seems, is the command to love our enemies. How is such a love possible?

Two things hinder us from understanding this commandment. The first is that we have not fulfilled the commandment that goes before: 'If any man will come after me, let him deny himself' (Matt. xvi. 24)—the commandment of spiritual poverty. Only by renouncing ourselves and all that belongs to us, our sympathies and antipathies, opinions, habits, views—only so can we understand the Gospels and, in particular, the commandment to love our enemies.

Secondly we must relinquish the notion that humanity is divided into two hostile camps, two different breeds of men: the just and the sinners—those predestined for beatitude and those doomed to perdition. This is not so. We are all sinful, all tainted with original sin, and our Lord suffered for all of us. He is the friend of sinners and warns those who consider themselves righteous that publicans and harlots will enter the kingdom of heaven before them. All are equally dear to Him, and it is to Him that the final judgement belongs. That is why Christ's words about love are directly followed by an admonition not to judge: 'Judge not, and ye shall not be judged' (Luke vi. 37). Judge not, and it will then be easier for you to love every man; judge not, and you will have no enemies. Look upon your 'enemies' as upon sick people, suffering from the same illness as yourself, on the point of perishing, just as you are. Abandon your personal judgement and look on things from the point of view of God's plan in the world. Remember that the good will undoubtedly end victorious, definitively and universally, leaving nothing to the devil.

†

The passing of time is terrifying as long as one remains motionless. We must plunge into the depths, where time is a matter of indifference.

†

The most acute sorrow for the deceased is sorrow for oneself, a selfish, personal pain. The righteous, the humble, the saintly know no sorrow.

†

To expect and to demand miracles is not only impious, inasmuch as it shows a lack of trust in God; it is also senseless, for we can count millions of miracles that have actually taken place, and if none of them has convinced us, why should we be convinced just by this one extra miracle?

†

We can live our entire life—and many in fact do—as a pale reflection and copy of someone else. The first and primary meaning of living is to be oneself, and from this to ascend to the transfiguration of oneself into the 'image and likeness of God'.

†

'Thou shalt not commit adultery': the word used in Slavonic—*prelyuby*—means a love which transgresses the law. Purity or im-

82

purity do not reside in a thing or deed in itself; but it is the shifting, the transgression which is impure. Manure in the field is the farmer's joy: it yields bread; but laid on the table, for instance, it is something revolting and out of place.

†

If 'the Father knoweth', why should we ask for anything, as we do in the Lord's Prayer and other prayers?

What matters in such prayers is our act of turning consciously to God, our humility, the feeling of connection and dependnece; and besides this, there is the importance of framing things explicitly in words, of communion.

†

On the destiny of non-Christians after death: 'For as many as have sinned without law shall also perish without law' (Rom. ii. 12). Does this mean that those who have *not* sinned 'without law' will be justified? For it is said (verse 15) that they 'shew the work of the law written in their hearts' and in their conscience.

†

A vow contains a partial acceptance of the suffering which has been sent us, and our acquiescence in regard to it: Lord, Thou sendest suffering in order to enlighten us; I pray Thee, replace this suffering by some other—may my child be cured, and I promise to bear the pain under another form: fasting, pilgrimage, or some other spiritual or physical sacrifice.

†

Sweat, tears, blood. . . . If sweat is accompanied by inner re-bellion, anger, murmuring; if tears are caused by pain, offence, rage; if blood is shed without faith—the soul will not obtain any benefit.

But if all this is accomplished in a spirit of obedience, con-trition, and faith, it purifies and elevates us.

†

Happiness is not an end in itself; it is the result of right living. If a life is correctly constructed, happiness will follow: and a correct life is a just life.

†

From a letter to a sick person:

Have you ever reflected, dear friend, on the words of Saint Paul: '. . . we faint not; but though our outward man perish, yet the inward man is renewed day by day. For our light affliction, which is but for a moment, worketh for us a far more exceeding and eternal weight of glory' (2 Cor. iv. 16–17). What is this mysterious link, stressed everywhere in the Gospels, between suffering and 'glory', that is, spiritual radiance, flowering, and strength? I have come to the conclusion that for every spiritual effort, for every voluntary (and even involuntary) privation, re-nunciation, sacrifice, and suffering, we immediately receive in exchange inward spiritual riches. The more we lose, the more we acquire. Woe to those who are happy, well fed, full of laughter—they will be impoverished and will reach complete spiritual indi-gence. The heroic soul instinctively seeks sacrifice, the occasion of suffering, and is spiritually fortified in trials. We must ask God to send us trials and almost feel sad when we live in security. Children who have grown up in comfort, pampered and with plenty of food, grow up spiritually empty. On the other hand, those who have known sickness and poverty, develop spiritually, 'for our light affliction, which is but for a moment, worketh for us a far more exceeding and eternal weight of glory'.

†

Many are shocked by what they regard as the prosaic and inappropriate custom of collecting money in church.

Woe to us, if we consider this from a worldly, commonplace point of view. Generally speaking, there are no commonplace, no tiresome or non-religious matters: as long as it is done in a Christian way, everything becomes deep and meaningful. It is not so much the thing itself that counts as our attitude towards it. Does it not often happen that a noble, holy subject is treated in a blasphemous or hypocritical way?

St. Paul, collecting alms for the Church, transporting gifts, writes about these things without the slightest doubt that he is accomplishing a holy work: those who give multiply thereby in their hearts the fruits of the Spirit; those who receive are moved by this very act to praise God and to be grateful, because their fellow Christians not only teach the Gospel with their tongues, but also fulfil its precepts in their hearts. If we are one body bound to one Head—to Christ—then how can we tolerate the presence amongst us of poor, hungry brothers? You must accept the collections in church as a test of your faith, your love, your patriotism. When you give money in these collections, it is an expression, not so much of your financial resources, as of the richness of your heart. Look carefully and see what sort of feeling appeals for help arouse in your heart. With the hands of thousands of orphans and invalids Christ Himself knocks at your heart; and you open the door and let Him in, and you know that it is He because you feel within you the joy experienced by all merciful hearts. God is able to help through a 'miracle' that is His own, but this miracle is accomplished through men. Blessed are those who become the 'servants of the miracle'.

†

Why must we offer alms to every passing beggar, without inquiring into his merits, and even when we know that he is undeserving? Apart from the fact that the man who gives is spiritually enriched, while whoever closes his heart and purse robs himself—apart from this, if we refuse alms, especially near church doors, we do great harm to the beggar, inciting him to anger, killing his faith, stirring up his hatred of the rich, the satiated, the pious.

†

There are people who, without apparently believing in God, 'live in a moral way, doing good'. This is for the most part a false morality and a false good, inwardly poisoned by a hidden vanity and pride. And if it is pure Good, these men 'touch God's garments', without realizing it and without knowing how to call on Him by name.

†

If we understand Our Lord's words about the signs of faith (Mark xvi. 17–18) to mean that every believer possesses *all* these signs, we may fall into complete dejection: for in that case it is clear that there is no faith in us. Perhaps we can find consolation in what St. Paul says about the various gifts of the Holy Spirit (1 Cor. xii. 8–9): 'For to one is given by the Spirit the word of wisdom; to another the word of knowledge . . . to another the gifts of healing . . .'.

†

Holiness and knowledge are given by the spirit of *sobornost*.[1] Ignorance and sin are the characteristics of isolated individuals. Only in the unity of the Church do we find these defects overcome. Man finds his true self in the Church alone: not in the helplessness of spiritual isolation but in the strength of his communion with his brothers and with his Saviour. The Church is a living organism, integrated by common love, forming an absolute unity in Christ of the living and the dead.

†

I distrust the fundamental method of all theological speculation (though it is the method of the Holy Fathers); all symmetrical constructions, hypotheses, etc. are achieved with an obvious strain. I would say frankly: if a theological truth seems logical, symmetrical, etc. to our sinful mind, this means that it is not the truth. I prefer to remain faithful to the absurdities of the Gospel, rather than trust in philosophical constructions which are the more suspect, the more attractive they are. Only dead bodies and outworn ideas have precise outlines; those that are alive, are encircled by a variable and ever changing aura, filled with radiance and the breath of life. All definition and fixation in our human plans restrict and freeze up this breath of life, are always incomplete, arbitrary, and therefore incorrect.

†

The Jews did not believe the testimonies of the Scriptures, though they possessed the testimony of Christ Himself, of St.

---

[1] This is the Russian word for 'catholicity': it is sometimes translated 'conciliarity'. This term *sobornost* signifies above all the unity of many persons in the one Body of Christ, the Church—a unity in which each individual retains full freedom and personal integrity, while at the same time sharing in the corporate and communal life of the whole.

John the Baptist, of Christ's own deeds, and finally the voice from heaven, the Father's testimony. They did not believe, 'because they did not have the love of God' in them (John v. 42). This is the secret of all unbelief: if there is no love of God, then neither the direct voice from Heaven ('hallucination') nor inner illumination ('psychosis, mania') nor the most genuine testimonies are of any use.

But where there is love of God, and when you know that your true life is in Him, no proofs are necessary, for *this very love is proof*. Even if the whole of philosophy, the rules of logic, and all the evidence were against it, I would still prefer to remain with my love, against logic, against all evidence. Faith is not evidence, it is a choice: you stand before life and death, damnation or blessing—'choose life, that both thou and thy seed may live' (Deut. xxx. 19).

†

Turning our eyes from the radiant scenes of the Gospel to ourselves, we are thrown into confusion. Not only do we not move mountains, we lack even the tranquillity, the stability, the joy, afforded by faith; depression, fear, a troubled heart are our normal condition. In our despair we often pray for some sort of proof, some trifling sign of God's presence near us—for the slightest hint of His loving care for us.

But to expect a proof of God's existence is to refuse to accomplish the heroic feat of faith.

God does not exercise constraint, does not use violence. Faith is an act of love, which chooses freely.

Yet, we may object, our Lord gave Thomas tangible evidence of His reality. But not even this would help a sinful soul: we may see and not believe, as did the Pharisees. We too know of miracles which happened in our days: miraculous cures, miracles in our family, incidents in our own life which cannot be explained otherwise than by a miracle. May God help us, then, to remember the innumerable manifestations of His love, so that we may attain to that confirmation in our faith which gives strength, joy, and peace.

†

How sad and incomplete maidenhood is, and what a plenitude of life is found in womanhood. No love affair is capable of replacing marriage. In love affairs people are seen in their splendour and blossoming, yet they are not themselves: a love affair projects a deceptive, exaggerated image of reality, and the life of both lovers is inevitably a pose, though an excusable and innocent one.

Only in marriage can human beings fully know one another—the miracle of feeling, touching, seeing another's personality—and this is as wonderful and as unique as the mystic's knowledge of God. It is for this reason that before marriage man hovers above life, observing it from without; only in marriage does he plunge into it, entering it through the personality of another. This delight in real knowledge and real life gives us a feeling of achieved plenitude and satisfaction which makes us richer and wiser.

And this fullness is made still deeper through the emergence from the two of us—fused and reconciled—of a third, our child.

But from this arise unsurmountable difficulties: instead of a complex fullness, there usually appears a mutual misunderstanding, protests, and an almost inevitable separation of that third one from us. The couple cannot become a perfect trinity. Why should this be so? Is this failure inevitable? Can we do anything to prevent it from happening? That which we have procreated is part of ourselves, our flesh and blood and soul. In a child we recognize our own habits, inclinations—whence then the disagreement, the breaking away? I think that a perfect couple will produce a perfect child, which will continue to develop further according to the laws of perfection. But if in the married life of the couple there is an unresolved conflict, a contradiction, the child will be the offspring of this contradiction and will prolong it. If we have reconciled our antagonism only externally and have not conquered it by rising to a new level, this will be reflected in the child.

Another explanation: in the child, together with the soul and body which it has received from us, there is something further, which is essential—a unique and inimitable personality with its own way in life.

†

In the education of children, the most important thing is that they should see their parents leading an intense interior life.

†

The philosophy of family quarrels: they often result from the wife's reproaches, borne reluctantly by the husband even though they may be deserved (pride). It is necessary to discover the original cause of these reproaches. They often come from the wife's desire to see her husband better than he is in reality, from her asking too much, that is to say from a kind of idealization. On these occasions, the wife becomes her husband's conscience and he should accept her rebukes as such. A man tends, especially in marriage, to let things slip, to be content with empirical facts. The wife tears him away from this and expects something more from her husband. In this sense, family discords, strange as it may seem, are proof that the marriage has been fulfilled (not only planned): and in the new human being, in which two persons have merged, the wife plays the role of conscience.

That is why quarrels between people who are close to each other are on occasion even useful: the fire of the quarrel burns up all the rubbish of resentment and misunderstanding, sometimes accumulated over a long period. A mutual explanation and confession is followed by a feeling of complete calm and serenity—everything has been clarified, nothing weighs on our mind. Then the highest gifts of the soul are freed; entering into communion with one another, we come to talk over the most wonderful things, we reach a full unity of soul and mind.

†

In marriage the festive joy of the first day should last for the whole of life; every day should be a feast day; every day husband and wife should appear to each other as new, extraordinary beings. The only way of achieving this: let both deepen their spiritual life, and strive hard in the task of self-development.

†

So precious in marriage is love alone, so dreadful is it to lose love—and sometimes it vanishes because of such trifles—that we must direct all our thoughts and efforts toward this goal (also toward the 'Divine'). Everything else will come by itself.

†

On marriage:
Thesis: marriage is an institution blessed by God: Cana of Galilee, 'be fruitful and multiply' (Gen. i. 28), the sacrament of marriage, the wedding ceremony. Everything is all right.
Antithesis: 'It is good for them if they abide even as I' (1 Cor. vii. 8); the hundred and forty and four thousand virgins 'which were redeemed from the earth' and 'were not defiled with women' (Rev. xiv. 3–4); 'eunuchs for the kingdom of heaven's sake' (Matt. xix. 12); absence of saints glorified for their family virtues.
Synthesis (but not a full one, for nothing is yet fulfilled for us, all is infected by sin, including matrimony): Adam and Eve were created before the fall; the 'Song of Songs'; the symbolism

of the Gospel: 'the marriage feast', the bridegroom and the bride—Christ and the Church, 'this is a great mystery' (Eph. v. 32).

†

The difficulty of personal relations between relatives, and in general in the family, is due to the fact that in the family (husband and wife, parents and children) there usually prevails a relationship of an instinctive, natural character, and if one of the members of the family leads a spiritual life, he fares badly. It has been said of this situation that 'a man's foes shall be they of his own household' (Matt. x. 36).

†

The false judgement, the estimate, either good or bad—but usually wrong—which nearly everyone makes in regard to kith and kin: this originates from our inability to be objective towards *our own*, from the physical and passionate interest in *our own* which leads to blindness and exaggeration.

†

When, because of the merits of one person, Christ says 'This day is salvation come to this house' (Luke xix. 9), these words mean that the eternal character of our earthly ties, the ties of blood, is recognized in the next world. The merits and sufferings of one person save his relations. How consoling and significant are these words, what an eternal value they give to our earthly life!

†

The distrust of the intellect, of philosophy and theology, that is common in our day, cannot in any way be justified from the Gospels or from the Fathers of the Church, who themselves reflected and reasoned a great deal – for instance, Gregory of Nyssa, Maximus the Confessor, the Cappadocians in general.[1] I cannot recall a single Father who feared the human intellect, reasoning, differences of opinion. It goes without saying that our intellectual activity must be inspired by the love of God, by a thirst for truth.

†

Theosis (deification): our professors speak so lightly of this. The heart of the matter is not whether this is a Christian idea – it is indeed Christian. The question is what path to follow in order to reach this *theosis*. Which is the best way for the Christian to enter into the life and culture around him?

1. Social and economic work. This is the easiest way of all. But there are also difficulties here: distraction, worldly-mindedness, lack of concentration.

2. Science, technology. This is much harder; scientific work ruins the spiritual life, turns us away from things spiritual.

3. The arts – most difficult of all, for this sphere is ambiguous, demoniac.

Participation in culture is, from one point of view, a compromise so far as the spiritual life is concerned. Is not the method of deifying the world from within – the way which St. Seraphim followed – a more sure course? Then everything else is transfigured as well.

†

---

[1] St. Gregory of Nyssa (died 394) and St. Maximus the Confessor (died 662): Greek Fathers.

The three Cappadocians are St. Gregory of Nyssa, his elder brother St. Basil the Great (died 379), and their close friend St. Gregory of Nazianzus, known in the Orthodox Church as Gregory the Theologian (died *ca.* 390). In their youth all three underwent an elaborate training in pagan philosophy, which they never disowned but used in the service of Christian theology.

What a tragedy is hidden in men's relations with God. We seek Him and suffer because we are separated from Him—though we know that He dwells within our souls—and at the same time we experience a sort of deadened feeling, a kind of inexorable petrification, by which we are hopelessly divided from Him.

†

Passion makes even an intelligent man stupid.

†

Pride = loneliness = outer darkness. Pride leads to ambition, to partiality, inability to judge oneself aright, and so to stupidity. Every proud man is stupid in his judgements, even if nature has endowed him with the mind of a genius. Conversely, the humble man is wise even though he may not be 'clever', for the essence of wisdom—a feeling for Truth and humility in its presence—is accessible to him.

†

Concerning non-resistance to evil—Tolstoy understood it externally, and in the name of this commandment of love, he brought about much disturbance and great evil, denying the institutions and the justice of the State, and inspiring an atmosphere of revolt. The ascetic conception is the accomplishment of this commandment in *individual morality*.

†

The purifying force and significance of suffering are immense. Our spiritual growth mostly depends on *how* we bear our sufferings. Courage in the face of them, readiness to accept them—these are

94

the signs of a 'correct' soul. But we must not seek sufferings, nor invent them.

†

We constantly come across worldy people, whose attitude to life is wholly exterior, who stand at a distance from the Church, who do not want to acknowledge *their* lack of understanding, *their* unpreparedness to receive the Truth, and who impute this lack of understanding to the Church, to the Truth itself. Our viewpoint as Orthodox, our approach to God, are not empirical—based on the evidence of the senses—nor are they derived from formal logic and reasoning. They are based on living experience, which grows according to the measure of our spiritual growth, and they are linked with prayer and with our moral life. 'Wisdom will not enter into a soul that deviseth evil' (Wisdom i. 4).

†

'We have defiled thy image, and are enslaved by lust.'[1] The delights of the world destroy spiritual life; they lead to the loss of cool sobriety of the spirit, of clarity of thought, of self-control; attention is dispersed, the will weakened, the personality debilitated, scattered, disordered.

†

The force of virginity—the radiance of unsquandered sex—is sublimated into the highest spiritual values. Purity is the condition and source of genuine creativity.

†

---

[1] Words from one of the prayers of Preparation before Holy Communion.

95

In the presence of a rich interior life, the powers of the sexual sphere are to a considerable degree converted into aesthetic, moral and other energies. But if this does not occur—as with the majority of European youth—what remains is sheer bestiality which, conversely, of itself absorbs every spark of the other and higher manifestations.

†

Our whole environment—our education from earliest childhood, 'the struggle for survival'—teaches us 'self-respect'. But if any of us can put himself in the place of the publican—and may God help us all to feel that way—let him rejoice, for he is that stray sheep, that lost piece of silver, for the sake of which Christ came; his salvation causes more joy in heaven than that of a hundred just souls.

†

All do not realize with equal seriousness the great significance for our spiritual life of meditation on the Lives of the Saints. Some go so far as to say: 'I have the Gospels; I have Christ—I need no intermediaries.' Some do not actually utter these self-assured words, but on the other hand neither do they appeal to the saints during periods of spiritual depression (and who has not had such experiences?). For what is a saint? A man like ourselves, but one who, having followed the right path, has found that which we all seek—God. Why, then, should we not study them and follow their example? Strictly speaking, we all share the same aim—sanctity—according to the measure of our powers.

†

It is a mistake simply to stifle or to put to sleep whatever is sinful in us; for the sin will remain and will put out new shoots, even if we pluck them up again and again.

A good plant must be grafted onto the evil one – that is, we must sublimate our sinfulness, transfiguring it into the higher spiritual states, of which our sinfulness was but a distortion. An example of this: St. Paul and all those who actively and consciously 'build up' their souls.

†

A common feature of proud men – to be indignant over the lies of others, to protest against injustice, to crusade for the re-establishment of truth. In their blindness, they do not notice that they themselves are entangled in lies, that they cannot stand the truth even in a weak solution, that the right to truth must be earned. They cannot bear to hear the truth about themselves; and can truth be told to one who is suffering from mental illness? What does truth matter to him? All truth about himself will only pour more water into the mill of his insanity.

†

Sorrows destroy our sins: 'Where there is no sorrow, there is no salvation' (St. Seraphim). Not only suffering sent by God, but all spiritual effort, every voluntary privation, every renunciation and sacrifice, are immediately converted into spiritual riches within us; the more we lose, the more we acquire. This is why it is hard for a rich man to enter the kingdom of heaven (Matt. xix. 23), because in his case there is no conversion of earthly, temporal, corruptible goods into heavenly and incorruptible ones. Courageous souls instinctively seek sacrifice and suffering, and fortify themselves through renunciation. We find this many times confirmed in the Gospels and in the Epistles, especially in St. Paul. Even non-Christian religions are aware of this fact: look at the tortures inflicted upon themselves by fakirs, yogi, dervishes—for them it is a matter of precise calculation.

God sends us sorrows—let us accept them courageously and wisely, growing spiritually and fortifying ourselves through them.

†

Each Lent, God grants me during confession one dominating thought. This year it is the love of Christ and the essential means of struggling against sin—prayer addressed to Him.

†

. . . It is so sad to part with Lent and with the Week of Easter. I am always grieved by the closing of the sanctuary gates on the Saturday of St. Thomas[1] and, in general, by the ending of Easter Week. They still sing 'Christ is risen', but everything becomes more difficult, as if the gates of the kingdom of heaven had really closed, those gates which have only just been opened in answer to our prayers and fasting. People plunge themselves once more with a sort of ravenousness into futile, worldly pursuits, and the churches become empty.

†

Only the first steps in the approach toward God are easy; the feeling that we have wings, the enthusiasm caused by the certainty that we are approaching God, are followed by a gradual cooling down, by doubt. In order to sustain our faith, it is necessary to make an effort, to struggle, to fight for it.

†

---

[1] The Saturday after Easter.

The beginning of the spiritual life is to emerge from subjectivity, from onself, to outgrow oneself by entering into communion with the highest principle—with God.

†

Death is occurring around us with such frequency that it has almost ceased to be frightening; at times it seems to me more real than life. And the greater the number of our dear ones that have passed on to the other side, the easier this passage becomes.

†

Why is the Church silent about the world beyond death? Man lives, thinks, and feels in the conditional forms of time and space. Outside these, we cannot think or speak.

The life beyond death is conditioned by different forms. If we try to speak of it, we shall speak in the language of earth. Hence the chaste silence of the Church.

†

Orthodoxy in particular is sensitive to the contrast between the 'spiritual beauty of the celestial world' and the beauty of 'this world'. We suffer from a sense of the darkness and sin which are mingled with everything in the world. In becoming Orthodox, we all become partly ascetics.

†

God created life.
The devil defeated it through death.
God repulsed the victory of death by Resurrection.

†

The entire modern world says: 'Sin!' Those who want to live by the law of light meet with opposition and they must not expect an easy, 'agreeable' life.

†

What are all our sins—I often think—compared with 'sinfulness'? But then, I argue, we allow ourselves to sin, and sin we do, yet we can also fight against sins; whereas 'sinfulness' is ours by nature and we have no control over it.

†

Difficulties when reading the Book of Job arise from the fact that the solution of the antinomies which Job raises is not sought where it should be: the heart of the matter is that Job's problems can only be solved by the advent of Christ.

†

The use of many words in prayer is helpful, if only because our consciousness is in this way fixed upon the holy words for a longer time. Even if we are not completely absorbed in the meaning of the words we utter, but only diverted from trifles, from vain agitation, worry, impure thoughts—even that is a great gain. And if we add to this a vivid sense of no more than one-hundredth of what we read, the soul acquires countless treasures.

†

The mysterious sphere of art—so attractive, so enchanting—affords its servants but little assistance in drawing nearer to what we call the truth; their usual characteristics are selfishness, pride, the thirst for fame, often extreme sensuality. In any case the sphere of art is not spiritual, but merely natural.

†

Why should priests not go to the theatre? The very principle of theatrical shows is rejected by the Church, which forbids masquerading, mumming, dressing up in the clothes of the opposite sex, all this being a sham, ambiguity, falsehood. Even to be no more than a spectator means that one is in a way taking part in it all. As regards the actor, the greater his passion in performing, the greater the harm he causes to his soul, allowing confusion and untruth to take up their abode in it.

†

Why do people of mixed blood feel Russian nationality so acutely? Dahl, Gershenzon, even Pushkin? Because the mixture of various bloods confers the faculty of seeing things in brilliant, stereoscopic relief.

†

I read about the cases of healing by Father John of Kronstadt,[1] and I feel puzzled: I am often inclined to consider sickness as the visitation of God, and I do not always find the courage to pray for the healing of the sick, so deeply do I acknowledge the hand and will of God in sickness. Is not the prayer for healing an intrusion into the destiny which is from God? But then, what is healing?

---

[1] Father John of Kronstadt (1829–1908), parish priest in a suburb of St. Petersburg, celebrated throughout Russia as a preacher and spiritual guide, and noted for his gifts of healing. He has already been proclaimed a saint by part of the Russian Church.

Perhaps the liberation from sin, through the prayers of the just, with healing as a result.

†

Absolution, the remission of sins, is given by God according to the measure of our repentance and faith.

†

How to distinguish genuine contrition from repentance of a formal type, which often deceives even the penitent himself? It is only necessary to agree with him, and if his contrition does not arise from the depths of his heart, instead of being penitent he begins to justify himself, feels displeased, and takes offence.

†

Every man has gone through the living and convincing experience of the struggle against sin, of the joy of victory gained over it, of the solace of good and prayer.

†

All of us have experienced a kind of enlightenment when we realize fully the vanity of our everyday life, when our soul is drawn towards purity and goodness as to a forsaken fatherland, wherein we seem to sense the breath of Christ's spirit. How is one to prolong those moments, to make them last a while, and so to transmit them to the people around us, to live and be nourished by them, seeking safety in them at times of weakness and dejection?

†

The youngest children of the family and the children of old age are usually the chosen ones: the Holy Virgin, John the Baptist, Isaac, Joseph; St. Teresa was the youngest of nine children. In fairy-tales, the youngest is marked out from the others, and what distinguishes him is precisely something spiritual. No doubt this arises from the fact that the physical, selfish, and passionate element has weakened in the parents, and the spiritual element has grown.

†

What we call actual reality is only half-real and not very actual. It is our attitude towards things that turns them into this or that, gives them finishing touches, converts them into good or evil. The same can be said of human beings. No one except God knows what they really are; more correctly speaking, human personality is something fluid, plastic; we fashion for ourselves an imaginary, schematized figure—often around some accidental feature—and then admire or abuse it. How much wiser are simple people—they do not invent a man, they take him as he is, and accept without protest the most discordant qualities.

†

. . . The swiftly flowing, irresistible, dancing current of the hours, days, years, often throws us into despair. We scarcely have time to live, to see our family. It is difficult to express my feeling —I am painfully aware both of the poignancy and strength of my love, and of its vanity, its torturing transiency.

†

Sometimes I observe a state of soul which, so far as outward signs are concerned, seems absolutely healthy—the person in question practices frequent and prolonged prayer, enjoys being in church, all his interests centre on his Church life. But at the same time he is stiff, unkind, loves no one. I can hardly understand it: I know of a kind of prayer after which the entire man is changed; but I think that such a prayer, 'isolated' from all else, is not a correct, salutary condition, for it contains only one element—the least important: form—but it lacks real, tangible results.

†

We have no grounds whatever for the expectation that God will reveal Himself to us—in our present state—in a full and absolutely convincing manner. But the words of the Apostle—'Every one that loveth . . . knoweth God . . . for God is love' (1 John iv. 7–8) —show us the path which we must follow.

†

Childlikeness is lost in life and regained in holiness.

†

Concerning an accident near Paris:

Every accident is a threat and a reminder: 'Except ye repent, ye shall all likewise perish' (Luke xiii. 5). Each accident is an ordeal to which our fidelity to God is submitted, an attempt on the part of the Devil to shake our faith. Our terror is largely the result of the imprisonment of our mind in the flesh. The world is full of blood and tears, and we, like small children, are terrified by the sight of two hundred dead. A train gone off its tracks, broken legs, arms, and skulls we regard as reality; whereas in fact all this is but illusion, a temporary state of being half-alive, for the fashion of this world passeth away. If we see this accident in its spiritual aspect, the souls of the children, and so on, we should not be afraid. If only the mothers could realize all this!

†

Man emerges from the infinite and returns to the infinite. How is it, then, that during their brief span of life almost all ordinary people have such great dread of everything that links them to the infinite, everything that extends beyond the common, narrow framework of everyday existence? Why do they build up their life as if deliberately leaving no room at all for anything spiritual?

†

The majority of the problems of life—sorrows, inner difficulties —of which one hears during confession, are due to the fact that men live outside the Church, yet appeal to the Church for the solution of their difficulties. They have no determination to change their life. They do not even give a thought to this—that is why the Church is helpless in such cases. Enter the Church, accept the entire order of Church life, and then the difficulties solve themselves.

†

The cult of the cross, the infamous instrument of execution, has recruited for Christianity men endowed with the utmost interior freedom.

†

Our entire life is built on the pattern of the Easter chants: on one side—the tomb, death, descent into hell; on the other side— resurrection, life, joy. 'For Thou hast descended into the tomb, O Thou who art immortal, yet Thou hast destroyed the power of hell.'

Fragments of a Diary

Our life's task is to let the elements of heaven and resurrection triumph over the forces of hell and death.

†

It is divine to love those who hate.
It is diabolical to hate and insult those who love.
It is human to love those who love, to hate those who hate.
But—'Be ye therefore perfect, even as your Father which is in heaven is perfect' (Matt. v. 48).

†

The feeling of extreme sinfulness is often, especially in youth, but another form of the passion of pride: 'I am extraordinary in everything, even my sins are deeper, more dazzling, than those of other men.'

†

'Refuse ye not one another, except it be with consent for a time, that ye may give yourselves to fasting and prayer' (1 Cor. vii. 5). . . . This is a recognition of the need for rhythm in the Christian life, for the alternation of fasting and prayer with ordinary life. This instruction is full of the deepest wisdom: the attempt to dwell on the heights of prayer without relaxation leads to depression and despair.

†

How shall we combine attentiveness to our own selves (in the ascetic sense) and the renunciation of ourselves? By paying attention to our sins, we renounce ourselves.

†

It is not the definition of sin that is important, nor its precise psychological description, nor even correct arguments concerning the sources and consequences of sin. No: the sense of the very *stuff* that sin is made of, of the nature of sin, of the pain and sorrow caused by it, the thirst for liberation from it—that is what is important.

†

We must not put our vices to sleep—we must uproot them. Here lies the advantage of life in the world: through conflict with other people and through situations which expose us to temptation, it reveals our own heart to us.

†

There are two kinds of men, so far as capacities for spiritual understanding, if not experience, are concerned.

In the case of the first, when conversing with them, our tongue sticks to the roof of our mouth, there is no echo, no response—just deafness and blindness. And these are nearly always people who are happy, well-fed, whose lives are well-organized. They have a sense of humour, are witty, good-natured.

But there are others who drink in every word about spiritual things, who understand the slightest hint, who are hard on themselves, capable of repentance and feeling, who are morbidly sensitive towards the sorrows of others—they are the sick, the unfortunate, the dying. I used to fear them, but now I am glad of every opportunity to be in precisely such company, and always learn a lesson from it. How many cases have I seen, when hopelessly sensual people, under the influence of sickness, became sensitive, spiritual, and responsive. Sometimes, however, the opposite takes place: a person somehow coarsens under the impact of misfortune. The reason is clear—a person avidly embraces life and happiness, placing it above everything else, above the Church,

God, the love of Christ; and so the misfortune which suddenly befalls him takes him unawares, embitters and coarsens him.

†

Sickness is not a misfortune but a lesson and a visitation of God: when St. Seraphim was ailing, he was visited by the Mother of God, and we too are visited by the supreme powers if we humbly accept our ailments.

†

We are all fortunate if only because of the fact that we belong to the Orthodox Church, which has taught us to pray, which has disclosed to us all the wisdom we are capable of receiving, and which continues to teach us, visibly or invisibly.

We know the Way and the Truth and the Life. How many great minds and hearts have suffered entanglement and perished, without having found truth; yet we possess it. Admittedly, some of us let go the rope for a time, like those who learn to swim, but even they know that there is but one path, and that everything else is self-indulgence and sin.

†

The man who lives outside God knows himself to be weak, full of contradictions, subject to sin and death. The world also appears to him thus enslaved, and at the same time he thirsts for the deification of himself as well as of the world.

This dramatic contradiction between the obvious limitations of the world and of mankind and man's desire for the Absolute is resolved by Christianity, which has satisfied all the cravings of the pre-Christian world. God, whom antiquity conceived anthropomorphically, who for the pagan religions was *all* and for Buddhism *nothing*, becomes in Christianity God-Love, who grants to man knowledge, freedom, strength and salvation.

†

Let us try to live in such a way that all our actions, our whole life may be, not a sleepy vegetation, but a development—as strong and deep as possible—of all our potentialities; and that this may take place, not some time in the future, but now, immediately, at every moment. Otherwise irresolute and slovenly living will inevitably give birth to an impotence and flabbiness of soul, an incapacity for faith and intense feeling; life will be squandered in vain, and we shall scarcely be able to rid ourselves of the cold scum which covers us—the fire of genuine heroism alone will then be able to consume it. . . .

†

We have already evidence enough to prove to us that the power exercised over humanity by Christian ideas is without precedent. This is acknowledged by the enemies of Christianity themselves. Nietzsche declared that the whole of humanity is 'corrupted' by Christianity, that human psychology and morality are entirely permeated by Christian 'decadence'. Rozanov,[1] before his conversion to Orthodoxy, affirmed with awe and gloom that men are incurably infected by that 'sweet poison', himself among them. We cannot say that after Christ all history became Christian; we know how far we are from this, today in particular; but we can claim that under the influence of Christian ideas history became *qualitatively* different. Dough rises under the action of yeast, yet does not become identical with yeast; wood burns under the action of fire, but the residue of ashes and cinders has nothing in common with fire. The same can be said of ideas, of their influence on

---

[1] Vasily Rozanov (1856–1919), Russian writer and religious thinker.

humanity. And such, too, has been the transfiguring action of the Christian religion on humanity.

Christianity has taught us to value in man, not his attributes and qualities, but his essential kernel – his soul; Christianity was the first to proclaim the absolute value and uniqueness of *every* human soul. It was also Christianity that succeeded in cleansing the human soul of all that is accidental and sinful, thus disclosing its infinite beauty and divine essence. All the world's riches are as nothing compared to this supreme value of the soul: 'For what is a man profited, if he shall gain the whole world, and lose his own soul?' (Matt. xvi. 26). Hence all the persuasive force of Christ's words, when he warns us against this or that vice which kills the soul. If man is so sacred, then every thoughtless action towards oneself or others is criminal, and to allow onself to commit such an action is to destroy this sacred element; every sin is a deep scar on a beautiful picture, a hideous wrinkle on an angelic face. Beware of sin – that is, protect yourself against corruption, destruction, against the death of the soul.

Just as trembling hands, inflamed eyes, a bent back, are the natural consequence of an ill-spent life, just as a weakened memory, senile weakness of the mind are the result of sin – even so a deeper decay of personality is caused by turning aside from the divine law. But what is the mystery of this preciousness of our 'self'? It lies – answers the New Testament – in the fact that we are the 'sons of God' (1 John iii. 2), that we are 'God's kin, God's race' (compare Acts xvii. 28). This doctrine of man's participation in Divinity, which is already found in Plato, came to life in Christianity and raised man's consciousness to unprecedented heights, opening before him radiant perspectives of the future through the commandment, 'Be ye therefore perfect, even as your Father which is in heaven is perfect' (Matt. v. 48).

†

The approach of light is terrifying and torturing for untruth and sin. The fear of God is the beginning of wisdom, the beginning of repentance, the beginning of salvation.

†

The feeble control which we exercise over our emotions, over the pieces of knowledge which we have acquired, results from our lack of religious culture. Hence the inner chaos of modern European minds, and the disciplined character of the minds of the East, where everything is based on religion. Without this, all efforts expended in self-development are fruitless.

†

It is not behaviour, words and actions, which are essential, but what fills our heart. The good deed is not the one which appears good, but which springs forth from the fullness of the merciful heart; it is the same with wicked words and deeds which are but the offshoot of a heart full of evil forces. To be good is not to be trained to do good actions, but to accumulate the warmth of grace in one's heart, above all through purification and prayer. In order not to suffer from the frost, we must be inwardly warm. How can we prevent ourselves from growing cold in the world? By enveloping our heart in the warmth of the grace of the Holy Spirit.

†

Prayer is an art; wrongly articulated prayer augments inner chaos, especially where persons with unstable nerves are concerned.

†

From the beginning of Lent I have been reading Isaac the Syrian. I am filled with admiration, moved, spiritually fed by him. I am filled with admiration by the force of his arguments, by his bold, effortless flight into the most secret spheres; I am moved by the loving-kindness, by the sacred love, with which his very style is infused; I am sustained by his wise advice, always precise and concrete, always expressed in a spirit of love. Yet at the same time I am filled with awe; he writes for monks, and he asks so much of them that he throws the lay reader into despair. What are we to hope for, we who are steeped in vain agitation, untruth, anger and passions? From monks he demands solitude; from hermits, silence; from those who observe silence, an entire abandonment to prayer, so that even the attention required for fetching water and collecting alms is a betrayal of God's task. Truly, our only hope is in God's mercy, and not in our works or merits, whatever they may be.

†

I bid a sad farewell to the end of Lent. In Lent how much good is accomplished with greater ease, how much evil loses its power and fades away, what joy there is in observing those who pray, fast, approach the holy Chalice with devotion! However frequent the disappointments and vexations during confession, however great the number of lazy, indifferent souls, blinded by sins and passions—there are yet many who possess a keenly sensitive conscience, who are merciless towards themselves, who love God and thirst for purification. Every confession is also a lesson and a spiritual gain for the priest who hears it.

†

In answer to the question whether those who approach the sacraments without sufficient contrition and faith are absolved of their sins, Bishop Innocent of Cherson says:[1] 'Without these things you will not receive absolution from God, no matter how often the priest repeats: forgiven, absolved.'

†

Lent strengthens the spirit of man. In Lent man goes out to meet the angels and the demons.

†

Cornelius the Centurion fasted up to the ninth hour, and then the angel appeared to him; the same happened to Peter (Acts x). Note the link between fasting and mystical gifts.

†

The circumstances with which our Lord has surrounded us are the first stage leading to the kingdom of heaven; and this is the only way of salvation possible for us. These circumstances will change as soon as we have profited by them, converting the bitterness of offences, insults, sickness, and labours into the gold of patience, forbearance, and meekness.

†

Even our good qualities are often turned into defects. For instance, indifference to money, to our position in the world, is sometimes not so much the result of our confidence in Divine Providence as of laziness and irresponsibility. Oblomov, too, was

---

[1] Innocent Borisov, Archbishop of Cherson (1800–57), the most famous Russian preacher of the nineteenth century.

indifferent to his career, and Stiva Oblonsky could seem disinterested in money matters.[1]

†

Our inner self is always in a bad state; God forbid that one fine day we should find that all fares well in our soul's economy. Its condition will remain unhealthy until God, in His infinite mercy, accepts us all—whether weak or strong, sick with sin or righteous—solely in virtue of our love for Him.

†

'Having eyes full of adultery, and that cannot cease from sin' (2 Peter ii. 14). 'Unceasing sin' can be counteracted by 'unceasing prayer' (1 Thess. v. 17).

†

'Insensibility', petrification, deadness of soul—these are the result of long-established sins which have not been confessed in time. The soul is greatly eased if we immediately confess the sin we have just committed, while we still feel its pang. Confession, if postponed, leads to insensibility.

†

'Neurasthenia', 'nervousness', and the like are, it seems to me, simply aspects of sin—namely, the sin of pride. The greatest neurasthenic of all is the devil. Can a humble, kind, patient

---

[1] Oblomov: hero of Goncharov's novel of that name. Stiva Oblonsky: a character in Tolstoy's *Anna Karenina*. Both are good-natured and generous, but with these characteristics go others less admirable—laziness, lack of will-power, weakness.

individual be imagined as a neurasthenic? And, conversely, why does neurasthenia inevitably express itself in anger, irritability, criticism of everyone except ourself; in intolerance, hatred of other men, extreme sensitivity with regard to all that concerns us personally?

†

The easy way in which we abandon our vantage-point—often won with difficulty—is truly frightful. It is enough for us to become aware of the slightest feeling of ill-will towards us, of the faintest reproach or mockery, and all our sympathy towards the person in question vanishes, leaving no trace. We are pleasant as long as people are pleasant to us. Yet this has nothing in common with what a genuine brotherly attitude towards men should be.

†

The ordinary year of a 'normal' Orthodox: a 'good' confession, a certain elation during half that day. The next day: he slips already, but stops and recollects himself. An hour (or a day) later, he sins again. He recollects himself, but with less energy. And so one thing succeeds another, till he shrugs his shoulders and sinks into a hopeless callousness for the rest of the year, till Lent comes round again. Then he once more takes himself in hand, remembers the impending devotions, and so on. Thus only six or seven days out of a whole year are given to God and to the spiritual life.

†

Concerning the act of reciting 'other people's prayers' (proudly contrasting them to 'our own' prayer): an example is offered us by Christ. His prayer and lamentations on the Cross are 'quotations' from the psalms: 'My God, my God, why hast Thou forsaken

115

me?' (Ps. xxii. 1) and 'Father, into Thy hands I commend my spirit' (Ps. xxxi. 5).

†

'For therein is the righteousness of God revealed from faith to faith' (Rom. i. 17)—an obvious affirmation of different gradations of faith.

†

Pia fraus of the Orthodox: the story of the monk-servant who reconciled through a lie two elders who had quarrelled. The advice of Father John of Kronstadt: not only to abstain from repeating evil judgements, but actually to communicate imaginary good ones. In general, the indifference of Orthodoxy to some kinds of untruth. In my opinion, this is the result of a certain contempt for the realities of life. Our squabbles, quarrels, anger—all these are 'non-existent' (though they do exist somehow), while the imaginary good (though imagined) is more real.

†

An enterprise begun in prayer cannot be anything but successful —because it is begun with love, hope, faith.

†

An argument for materialists and atheists: religion is *useful* for the soul and even for the body. Spiritual peace is the best remedy for every kind of sickness—and it is given only by religion.

†

Many divine truths are beyond our understanding—but their very inconceivableness, their incomprehensibility, is their attribute. In order to grasp them wholly with our limited human consciousness, we must ourselves become equal to them, become divine.

†

In our present life everything is so uncertain, insecure, painful, almost intolerable, that death in no way appears as something terrifying. I often think of death as a calm and luminous haven, where there is no sickness, no sadness and, in particular, no parting. When, during morning and evening prayers, I pray for my loved ones in minutes of sadness, I am almost glad to think that I will soon be with them, and *their* life seems more certain than our phantom existence.

†

It is always best to overcome doubt and misfortunes, not by evading them or brushing them aside, but by passing *through* them.

†

If we divide up our misfortunes into separate moments of time, then sometimes misfortune does not appear in a single one of them.

†

Nature, or more correctly speaking, the Providence of God, dictates to each time of life its own spiritual regimen. With the approach of old age, our bodily capacities decrease and the conditions favourable to a concentrated interior life increase: there is less activity and more time for prayers; the organs of our exterior senses are blunted; there is less distraction, and more attention is given to our inner world; a diminished ability to digest heavy, fattening food – hence, a natural disposition to fasting; enforced chastity. Blessed is he who understands these signs and goes out to meet God's loving care on our behalf; blessed is he who, in the construction of his life, gradually replaces corruptible building materials by fireproof and indestructible ones.

†

Often, the most cruel self-chastisement and explosions of repentance vanish as soon as the confessor priest admits the penitent's sinfulness. In this way it is possible to discover the source of the repentance – whether it is genuine or only a hysterical pleasure in uncovering of one's own self, even if this is accompanied by a willingness to accuse oneself of sin.

†

'While we are at home in the body, we are absent from the Lord: for we walk by faith, not by sight' – *per fidem . . . et non per speciem* (2 Cor. v. 6–7). How 'absent' can we be? Is it possible for us to be entirely absent? Do we sit in the shadow of death, in the infernal regions? This is my habitual feeling, my constant grief. The only way out is in the sacraments, in prayer.

†

My constant thought – God's inaccessibility, His infinite distance from us. Even when we approach the Holy Eucharist, when we receive the divine Body and Blood, God continues to dwell in other worlds, hopelessly far from us. The Holy Virgin alone – 'one of us', of 'our own race' – rose with great ease above the seraphim; and this was before the Incarnation of Christ. This means that there is a possibility of nearness. It is probable that only children, only the most childlike, are close to God. But what of the others?

Why are such superhuman efforts necessary (as in the case of the ascetics), in order that one out of a million may behold the angels, converse with God, pray and obtain an answer? Whence this stubborn opacity, impenetrable to God, to the Holy Eucharist, to Christ's sacrifice, to His Love?

†

Concentration on self—auto-eroticism—is the beginning of all sin.

†

Laughter (not smiling) weakens man spiritually.[1]

†

Is there in me—however bad I am—anything that will consciously oppose itself to Christ when He comes in all His Glory? Will not every human soul rush headlong towards Him, welcoming him as one long-expected and desired?

†

The list of the dead to be prayed for, drawn up by nannies, contains scores of names (certainly their entire village), while the educated list five or six names.

†

Our tolerance towards those who belong to other religions, and in general our tolerance towards differences in theological opinion,

---

[1] To most western readers, Father Alexander's teaching here cannot but seem unduly severe. The same attitude towards laughter, however, is characteristic of a whole series of eastern spiritual writers. Possibly what they have in mind is primarily laughter of a harsh and mocking character—laughter *at* rather than *with* a person. No doubt they are thinking also of the helplessness, the essential lack of self-control, which is a feature of all violent laughter.

should first of all receive nourishment from the Gospels and the Church: for the Christianity of St. John is not wholly identical with the Christianity of St. Peter, and that of St. Francis of Assisi is not that of Paul the Apostle. The same applies to different lands and peoples. The fullness of Truth is something absolute, and therefore incompatible with the world; the world and man are essentially limited, and therefore accept the truth of Christianity in a limited way. And because each people and each individual man is limited in a particular way, each comes to have a distinctive conception of Christianity: yet fundamentally the Christianity of all alike remains the same. The gifts of the Spirit also vary both among individual men and among peoples.

†

Among all the Christian faiths, none has a more vivid feeling of a *personal* Christ than has Orthodoxy.

In the Protestant faith, this image is distant and has no personal character. In Catholicism, it is outside the world, and outside the human heart. The Catholic saints behold Him *in front* of their eyes, as a model whom they seek to imitate, even to the point of receiving the stigmata, the wounds caused by the nails. The Orthodox alone—not only the saint, but the ordinary pious layman—feels Him inside himself, in his heart. This intimacy with God has nothing in common with western exaggeration and sentimentality, and the soberness of Orthodox religious feeling excludes all romanticism and affectation. In Orthodoxy, the Russian religious feeling happily escaped both rationalism—towards which Russian common sense might have been attracted—and the unbridled mysticism towards which it might have drifted, as a result of that trait in Russian nature which Dostoyevsky defined as a tendency to overstep the limits and to peer into abysses. And yet these traits have in some measure remained in the Russian character, and explain the existence of numerous sects in the Russian Church. These sects are precisely divided into two groups, corresponding to these two peculiarities of the Russian character.

†

On Protestantism and Orthodoxy: in the little things they have, they have obtained very great results, and we, who have very great things, vegetate in mediocrity.

†

It is not ideas which are important, but facts and realities. Christianity rests on facts, which one must either repudiate with sufficient grounds or accept with all their implications.

These facts are of a twofold kind:

1. Christ, His life, death and resurrection, as described in the Gospels. To repudiate all this, to consider the Evangelists as liars and conscious impostors, is extremely difficult. It is no less difficult to consider them as visionaries and victims of fantasy. If we read the Gospel stories carefully, especially the story of the Resurrection, if we read them without prejudice, with an unbiased mind and a free soul, it is impossible not to see that all this actually happened; it is the simplest and most natural hypothesis.

2. The second group of facts—the life, feelings, miracles and prayers of the saints and of the ordinary faithful, the fact of the extraordinary blossoming of human beings in Christianity, their overcoming of sickness, old age and death, the transfiguration of their souls: this is clearly shown in the life of every saint. Can one provide a scientific explanation for the facts found in the life of St. Seraphim of Sarov, of St. Francis of Assisi or John of Kronstadt? Is it not a miracle that the ancient world, the world of that time, weary, corrupt and senile, so rapidly acquired the youthful, fresh forces of Christianity? Yes, indeed, the phenomenon of Christianity is a miracle of God's power.

Christianity conquered the world without violence, it educated the youthful peoples, created the Christian culture by which we live up to this very day; it softened the usages in courts of justice, in social relations, it raised the dignity of woman, created Christian arts and sciences. And we are the legitimate heirs of this wealth. But we are not always aware of being heirs. A thin thread, ready to break, binds us to the Church. Let us try to renew within ourselves the thought of our 'birth in grace', of the dignity of our Christian calling. For Christians are a special race of men—'By this shall all men know that ye are my disciples, if ye have love one to another' (John xiii. 35). That is what we must be, despite all our poverty.

†

Questions to be offered for meditation to unrepentant sinners, before confession (whilst they say to themselves: 'And after all, what do my sins amount to? I have committed no special sins!').

1. Why did the saints consider themselves as the greatest of all sinners?

2. What is the meaning of the words: 'Be ye therefore perfect, even as your Father which is in heaven is perfect' (Matt. v. 48)?

3. 'Behold, He put no trust in His servants; and His angels he charged with folly' (Job. iv. 18).

†

Why does the sinner not appear repulsive to the priest who hears the confession, no matter how repulsive his sins? Because in the sacrament of repentance the priest observes a complete separation of the sinner from his sins (if the sinner is truly repentant).

†

Not all sick men can face a serious operation, not all those who confess their sins are capable of facing a real confession. Just as an operation—even if it is indispensable—can kill the patient, so the spectacle of his sinfulness, if suddenly called up from the depths of his soul, can deal a deadly blow to a man. One has to be indulgent and to feed the patient with fortifying medicine, until the right moment comes.

†

The rule of James Lange for the spiritual life:

We must have recourse to certain words, gestures, signs (the sign of the cross, bows, genuflections), in order to awaken and maintain a religious disposition in ourselves.

But, it might be objected, what is this disposition worth, if it is merely the result of artificial and exterior methods?

Bodily and psychic processes are closely linked and mutually influence each other. There is nothing humiliating in the fact that the spiritual life is influenced, not by any and every kind of sign, but by pious and symbolical attitudes and gestures. Our entire body, its form and outline, are not accidental—'I am the image of Thine ineffable glory'[1]—and sacred and symbolical expressions and gestures create lofty spiritual dispositions in the soul.

†

The essence of spiritual blindness consists in the fact of not seeing the Truth. It has different aspects—there is the blindness of a man loaded with a burden of drunkenness, gluttony, worldly worries, the blindness of fornicators, harlots, sinners; and there is that other kind of blindness—of Saul, of Christ's disciples; and there is the blindness of the Pharisees. The first two are caused by

---

[1] Words sung at the Orthodox funeral service.

ignorance, and especially by erroneous, deeply rooted opinions, also by sensual passions which obscure our inner sight; and the third is caused by pride. The first and the second attain salvation; the third perish.

†

The smallest particle of good realized and applied to life, a single vivid experience of love, will advance us much farther, will far more surely protect our souls from evil, than the most arduous *struggle* against sin, than resistance to sin by the severest ascetic methods of chaining the dark passions within us.

†

Garrulousness is due essentially on one hand to the absence of humility and on the other to a kind of primitive instinct which makes us delight in self-revelation, in pouring ourselves out like a bubbling stream. This immediately leads to a lowering of our spiritual standard, to an easy-going, loose way of life, to inner weakening and absentmindedness. We must struggle against it by a continuous wakefulness, by teaching ourselves to attribute a spiritual meaning to everything around us, by taking a serious spiritual interest in the person we are talking to.

†

'And when one member suffers, all the members suffer with it' (1 Cor. xii. 26) is said of the Church. If we do not feel this, we are not within the Church.

†

'I seek for truth.' Happy is he who places the accent on the last word: 'Truth'. It is far worse in the case of those who proudly emphasize the word 'seek', and are full of vanity because they are numbered among those who aim continually at the truth—'Ever learning, and never able to come to the knowledge of the truth' (2 Tim. iii. 7). But what is really bad, and occurs most often, is when the accent is placed on the 'I'.

†

The effort expended in securing control over ourselves and over our anarchic and autonomous nervous systems is greatly facilitated, and made quite easy, by the correct balance of our attention and imagination. We shall inevitably continue to stumble over every trifling obstacle until what is not a trifle has become sharply defined, vivid and convincing in our soul; until we strive with all our soul, heart, and mind towards what is essential, relegating to their proper place the trifles that poison our everyday life.

There are three stages in the struggle against 'nerves'—medical treatment, self-control and, most important of all, the building up of the highest values in the soul.

†

One must be careful to avoid nervous over-emphasis and declamation when reading in church. The prescribed style—its monotony, its modulations which do not stress any special point, which place the listeners face to face with the sacred words—is a manifestation of the very freedom of Orthodoxy: the reader, the priest, do not seek to draw anyone after them, do not impose their own interpretation—for perhaps there is no single meaning, but an infinite variety.

†

Often the words of psalms and prayers do not touch us, their inner meaning seems strange and incomprehensible to us. And this is quite natural, for the whole setting and structure of our life—outwardly well-organized and inwardly empty—have so very little in common with the deserts and monasteries in which the prayers were composed, with the spirit which inspired them. At rare moments—in great affliction, in solitude, if we escape for a time from the bonds of the world—there arises from our heart, as if it were our very own, the cry of lamentation: 'O Lord, come to my help!' Then we understand the experience of the man of silence and the recluse.

†

A good course for those of us who are unable to perceive our own sins is to observe what sins our friends and relations notice in us and reproach us for. This will nearly always serve as a correct indication of our real defects.

†

Does the soul fall asleep after death, does it or does it not remain in a state of slumber until the Day of Judgement? Subjectively speaking this makes no difference: in both cases we can say that the Final Judgement comes to the deceased immediately after death; for during this period between death and resurrection the consciousness probably does not function.

†

The cult of the dead—the most primitive form of religion—is also the most striking religious observance still to survive in a godless Europe. The celebration of All Souls Day comprises the minimum spiritual life of the average European.

†

Neither our natural attachment to life nor our courage in

bearing suffering, neither earthly wisdom nor even faith—however great—none of these can preserve us from sorrow for the dead. Death is a twofold phenomenon: there is the death of the departed, and the suffering and deadening in our own soul, occasioned by this painful process of separation. But the path of hopeless sorrow, gloom, and despondency is forbidden to the Christian. He must not recoil when faced with suffering nor remain impotently passive before it. He must exert his spiritual powers to the utmost in order to pass *through* suffering, and to emerge from it stronger, deeper, wiser.

No matter if we are weak in our faith and unstable in our spiritual life—the love we bear towards the departed is not weak; and our sorrow is so deep, precisely because our love is so strong. Through the tension of our love, we too shall cross the fatal threshold which they have crossed. By an effort of our imagination, let us enter into the world which they have entered; let us give more place in our life to that which has now become their life; and slowly, imperceptibly, our sorrow will be turned into joy which no man can take from us.

†

Conversation with X about fasting.

X: What is the basis for the division between foods which are forbidden and foods which are permitted in Lent? Why can we eat fish but not beef?

Answer: In deciding which foods can be eaten in Lent, the Church is not guided by sentimental considerations, like vegetarianism or Hinduism. The considerations are purely physiological—foods that 'fatten' or excite are forbidden.

X: Fasting has a deplorable effect on me: I grow weak, incapable of work, my normal state of mind depends entirely on whether I am hungry or not. I do not understand, therefore, why we should wear ourselves out in this way.

Answer: I will give you an explanation if you tell me first whether you make a clear distinction between the sphere of the soul and that of the spirit.

X: No, I do not understand this distinction clearly.

Answer: Well then, you cannot assert for sure that physical exhaustion is harmful to the spiritual life (as distinct from the life of the soul). I can give you examples to show that its effect is just the opposite—fasting develops spiritual powers: you cannot pray after a large meal; you do not visit the dying after drinking champagne; you console those who suffer better if you are not surfeited with food.

X: But this was all very well when our life was entirely adapted to the life of the Church. But today we have to fast without altering our usual work and our relations with other people; as a result our work suffers and we become irritable. When we fast, we should retire to a monastery and get away from our normal routine.

Answer: Do not be a perfectionist, and do not put off fulfilling the Church's commandments until the return of the conditions of the seventeenth century. You can achieve many things even now. Example: our nannies, servants, peasants.

X: That is not a very good example. I have never seen servants so bad tempered as during the last days of Holy Week. Clearly fasting has a very bad effect on the nerves.

Answer: You are quite right. But fasting is a completely external, technical, subsidiary exercise. If it is not accompanied by prayer and an increased spiritual life, it merely leads to a heightened state of irritability. It is natural that servants who took their fasting seriously and who were forced to work hard during Lent, while not being allowed to go to church, were angry and irritable.

†

The meaning of fasting:

Obedience to the Church.

Lightening of the body: 'The thoughts of mortal men are timorous and their devices are prone to fail. For a corruptible body weigheth down the soul' (Wisdom ix. 14–15).

Exercise of the will, self-control, renunciation, sacrifice.

†

The common view of fasting is a radical misapprehension. The important element in fasting is not the fact of *abstaining* from this or that, or of *depriving* oneself of something by way of punishment. Fasting is but a tested method for attaining certain necessary results: through fasting we weaken the body, in order to achieve a refinement of our spiritual, mystical capacities which were obstructed by the flesh, and thus to facilitate our approach to God.

In fasting—as in narcosis, intoxication, sleep—man reveals himself; some manifest the highest talents of the spirit, others only become irritable and bad-tempered. Fasting reveals the true nature of a man.

†

A work that is planned correctly and in a religious way, cannot lead to fatigue, neurasthenia or heart disease. If these symptoms exist, it is proof that a man is working 'in his own name'—trusting his *own* strength, his own charm, eloquence, kindness, and not the grace of God.

There are correctly pitched voices, and in just the same way there are correctly pitched souls. Caruso sang without fatigue, Pushkin would never have said that the writing of poetry was fatiguing; the nightingale sings all night, and when day breaks, its voice is still untired.

If we are fatigued by our work, by our relations with other

people, by conversation or prayer, this means only that our soul is incorrectly pitched. There are voices naturally 'pitched'; others are forced to seek the same results through prolonged effort and special exercises. The same can be said of the soul.

†

Illness and wisdom: in order to convince Eudoxius the Rhetorician that he is fitted by nature for philosophical studies, Plato appeals to the following features: nobility of soul, a gentle spirit, delicate health and physical weakness. All this appears to Plato of no little importance for the 'love for wisdom'.

†

The pattern of our relations towards our fellow men often appears to be the following: a person pleases us, we sincerely idealize him, we see nothing bad in him; and then, suddenly, the person in question fails us in this or that, lies or brags, proves cowardly, or betrays us. So we start to reassess his value, we erase everything that we saw in him before (and which nevertheless really was there), and throw him out of our heart. I have long recognized that this is a wrong and sinful method of human relationship. At the basis of such an attitude towards our fellow men lie two ideas of which we are not ourselves conscious: (1) I myself am untouched by sin; and (2) the person on whom I have bestowed my love is also sinless. How can we otherwise explain our severe condemnation of others and our surprise if a good, kind, pious person commits a sin? Such are the conclusions I draw from sad reflections concerning my own heart, and from my conviction that I myself am capable of all kinds of sins.

And yet, the rule which should govern our attitude towards our fellows is to forgive endlessly, for we ourselves are in need of endless forgiveness. It is essential not to forget that the good which we valued in someone is still there; as for the sin, it was always present, but we did not notice it.

†

In dreams we sometimes experience exalted and intense states of prayer, emotion, and joy, such as we are almost incapable of in our waking hours. Cannot this be explained by the passive condition of our body in sleep? It presents no obstacle.

†

The life of the body and the life of the soul vary in inverse proportion: thought kills emotion, intense thought kills the body.

†

N's letter about the beautiful, new, empty church, just completed: 'There is scarcely any congregation.' It seems increasingly evident to me that our decorative, pompous rites must end—inwardly, indeed, their end has already come. They are artificial and unnecessary; they have ceased to nourish the thirsting soul and must be replaced by different, more active and 'warmer' forms of religious communion.

How little our rites—with the priest separated from the faithful by the wall of the iconostasis, with the freezing space of inlaid floor between the congregation and the Holy Table, with the coolness shown by the 'visitors'—the faithful—towards each other, with the chalice presented in vain while the people stubbornly refuse to approach it—how little all this resembles the gatherings for worship in the age of the Apostles and the martyrs! The religious element languishes, while the scenic effects rise higher and higher; the flame in men's souls dies away, while the gilded ornaments and electric chandeliers grow brighter.

†

Standing in church, even when we are lazy and absent-minded, is not fruitless; if we look inside ourselves as we stand in this way, we shall perceive that at such a moment we are capable of much good, and can more easily refrain from evil; it is easier to forgive and to keep our heart at peace.

†

Despite the thousand obstacles arising from our distracted and futile way of life, having overcome the languidness and sloth of our soul, at last we manage to approach the Holy Chalice, and our Lord receives us as 'communicants', participants in the Holy Supper. This participation and communion are a great joy and a great source of strength. But we must not deceive ourselves. After the Last Supper the severest temptations awaited Christ's disciples: before their very eyes the Divine Master whom they had recognized to be the Christ, the Messiah, the future king of Israel and of the world, the Son of God, was seized, subjected to a humiliating trial, tortured and publicly executed as a criminal in the company of thieves, thus demonstrating His helplessness in the face of human wickedness. And only after having passed through this temptation did the disciples become worthy of the dazzling light of Holy Easter.

We too meet temptation when we leave the church, warmed by our prayers and by the prayers of those who have prayed there before us, and emerge into the darkness and cold of the outside world. The temptations of that outside world and the greatest temptations of all—those within our own soul—are waiting for us.

May Christ, to whom we are bound by the closest ties, help

us to overcome and to remain victorious over these temptations, and to preserve our joy until next Easter, and even until that Easter when we shall taste the new wine in the day of the kingdom of heaven that shall have no evening.

†

I think that the Church must rid itself of the dead weight of unbelievers and those of little faith (as has happened in Russia); it must gather itself together, cleanse itself of alien elements; and this will increase its radiance.

†

It is not so much Christianity that has absorbed paganism, as the world which has kept its paganism even after being converted to Christianity.

†

Here on earth, we already have both heaven and hell—in our passions, in our experience of what is good.

†

Do our merits justify us before God?

Even if our truthfulness, our good actions, our acts of heroism, are really great, what are they compared to God's Truth, what is our light compared to the inaccessible light of God's Glory, what is our beauty compared to the incorruptible beauty of the garden of Eden? It is merely a question of a little more or a little less, just as terrestrial distances—whether two miles or two million— are as nothing compared to the distances in the world of stars.

What is important is not the quantity of our good actions but the direction followed in our lives: to the right or to the left, plus or minus, towards good or evil, God or darkness.

†

The moment man accepts with gratitude the suffering which God sends him, he immediately emerges from its depths into such peace and happiness, that all around him experience relief and joy. It is enough to desire this, and God will grant it.

†

Life is a painful trial, and our misfortunes will always be with us until death: the Christian will never know idyllic happiness and comfort. But on the other hand the joys of 'this world' cannot be compared to the joy which God sends to the Christian.

†

Very often our misfortunes seem enormous because we magnify them in a quite unnecessary way: we expect the disaster before it has actually come; we imagine its effects on the hearts of our kin; in the intervals between moments of real suffering we go on suffering through inertia; we dwell on the memory of recently experienced pain. If we live in an Orthodox way, experiencing every moment of life in its fullness, misfortune will be rendered considerably less harmful, if it is not entirely overcome.

†

How can bodily states react on the spirit? How can religious gestures, the sign of the cross, the repetition of sacred words, move our soul to action? Normally the engine of a car puts the wheels into motion by itself: but there are occasions when a weak, defective motor cannot start working unless we first push the car and set the wheels turning.

†

Every sort of prayer is valuable, even inattentive prayer. The power and action of the word are independent of the psychological state of the person who utters it. If an injurious or obscene word pollutes and wounds the soul both of him who speaks and of him who hears, the sacred words of prayer, even if repeated absent-mindedly, cover our memory, mind, and heart with a delicate network, and have a beneficial effect on us of which we ourselves are unaware.

†

The world is crooked and God straightens it. That is why Christ suffered (and still suffers), as well as all the martyrs, confessors, and saints—and we who love Christ cannot but suffer as well.

†

'I behold our beauty, created in the image of God, lying in the grave.'[1] Against the ascetics who speak of the corruptness of our bodies, of the valueless, temporary nature of human beauty: it is not beauty that is temporary (for it is made 'in the image of God'), but our body.

†

Our life upon earth is a semblance, a reflection of life invisible,

---

[1] Words sung at the Orthodox funeral service.

and we must lead here, not that over-simplified, unconsecrated, external life that is usual for us, but a full, genuine life, indissolubly linked to the Divine life and sharing its nature. This applies not only to all the really important things, but likewise to all those things which are of secondary significance; it involves everything from our attitude to God to our most insignificant word or deed. This is particularly true in the case of marriage: what men have reduced to a mere physiological act invested with custom and ritual is in reality the highest disclosure of human personality, the achievement of plenitude in the mysterious union of two beings which the Apostle compares to that of Christ with the Church.

†

X writes to me: 'Subjectively I am very close to religion. I need it—the Church and all the rest. But what is important is the Objective; and this I have never felt.' What can one say about this? First of all: there is a difference between faith and knowledge.

A direct communication with God was given to Moses, to the saints, at rare moments. In this sense, our faith is no more than faith in (and knowledge of) their faith.

But if—an impossible proposition—there were no saints and we had not even a single certain case of communication with God (and we have thousands of such cases)—even so, each of us has had an experience of such communication, an experience which may be feeble because of our frailty, but which is none the less certain.

When we speak of communication with God, either we *know* what we are talking about or else we are talking nonsense. Speaking of God we invest Him with two attributes—a formal one, that He exists objectively, and a real one—that He is Love.

'And hereby we do know that we know Him, if we keep His commandments'; 'hereby know we that we are in Him'; 'he that loveth his brother abideth in the light'; 'every one that loveth . . . knoweth God . . .', 'for God is love'. All this from the First Epistle of St. John (ii. 3, 5, 10; iv. 7, 8).

It is totally unjustified to expect God to reveal Himself indubitably and fully to us as we are at the present moment. But in these words of the holy Apostle we are given the guiding thread which we must follow to approach near to God. There is no other way.

Moreover, it is impossible to reject the entire Gospel, Christ's miracles and teaching, His consciousness of being the Son of God, His Transfiguration, Resurrection and Ascension, the visible and objective descent of the Holy Spirit on the Apostles, and the entire multitude of saints that followed. We shall have either to adopt the trivial and philosophically lame standpoint of rejecting all this or else, recognizing the objectivity and reality of all the cases of Theophany, to ask ourselves: 'Why is it so difficult for me to accept all this?' The answer to the question is clear.

Has there been in my life, as in so many others, a clear, indubitable encounter with the Objective? Frankly, I must answer: no. But there have been many partial contacts: in certain rare instances of love expressed in entire self-denial; sometimes in prayer, especially during the holy service, you feel that you come out of yourself, that something which is not yourself has entered into you; in many situations, which cannot be explained except in terms of God's manifest help. This is faith no longer—it is knowledge, precise and comprehensible signals from the other world. All the rest is faith, assisted by the love of God.

†

Our special cross is that we are so distant in time from the days of Christ. But 'blessed are they that have not seen, and yet have believed' (John xx. 29). How difficult is the path leading to Christ, now that we see neither Christ nor those who have just seen Christ; when we scarcely even see people who really love Christ. To think that we could—but for the separation in time— have seen Christ with our own eyes, could have heard Him speak, and listened to the preaching of Paul and Peter!

†

A subject of my constant reflections and observation: the psychology of sin or, to be more correct, the psychic mechanism of fallen man. Intuition is replaced by rational processes; a fusion with objects, by five blind senses (truly 'external'); a grasping of the whole, by analysis. Primitive men with powerful instincts, incapable of analysis and logic, are much closer to the image of Eden. How sinful is the process to which we subject children, developing in them all the traits of the fallen soul.

†

Why is faith so difficult for man to achieve? Whence these doubts and periods of falling away? Why does faith at times withdraw from us completely, though we would give everything to retain it? First, this is a direct temptation of the devil. It would be extraordinary if we were not so tempted when something essential to us is involved. Secondly, we often want and expect a proof; this means a retreat from the heroism of faith and a search for direct knowledge. And yet, each of us has an *experience* of faith, however small, an experience of its life-giving effect on us; and to this experience we must hold fast.

†

People are capable of a deep understanding of life; they can distinguish with great *finesse* many a trait in the souls of others— but how rarely (hardly ever) does a man see himself. Here the keenest sight is dimmed and becomes prejudiced. We are excessively indulgent towards all the evil in ourselves, and immensely exaggerate every glimpse of good. I do not even mean that we should be stricter towards ourselves than towards others (though this is, as a matter of fact, required of us); but if we simply applied to ourselves the measure we use for others—even this would open our eyes in more ways than one. But we completely refuse to do so; we have become incapable of seeing ourselves and live in a state of blind security; yet our spiritual life has not even begun to develop, and cannot develop before we have abandoned this false attitude.

†

If we enjoy friendship with someone, and not only friendship but simply friendly relations, before severing them because of some misunderstanding, we should apply the rule of Jesus, son of Sirach, however *obvious* the friend's fault.

Ecclesiasticus xix:

13. Reprove a friend; it may be he did it not: and if he did something, that he may do it no more.

14. Reprove thy neighbour; it may be he said it not; and if he hath said it, that he may not say it again.

16. There is one that slippeth, and not from the heart: and who is he that hath not sinned with his tongue?

17. Reprove thy neighbour before thou threaten him; and give place to the law of the Most High.

The last rule is especially important—who has not sinned in words? How often we say angry, offensive, untrue words in a moment of irritation, cowardliness, frivolousness, weakness, or when possessed by some other sin—who can consider himself free from these sins?

†

How can we love our enemies? We are invulnerable to evil when we wear the armour of the Spirit, when the wickedness of men cannot reach us, when we gaze with love and pity on those who do us wrong. It is like being exposed to frost when the body is inwardly warm—for instance, after skiing. This state of complete absence of anger should not be confused with a conceited 'steel plating' of oneself against the world.

†

Analysis of repentance: pain caused by sin, repulsion felt towards it, its acknowledgement, confession, the firm resolution to be rid of it, the mysterious transfiguration of man, accompanied by tears, by a shock extending through the whole organism, by the purification of all the strata of the soul, the feeling of relief, joy, peace.

†

Nothing in life is accidental. Whoever believes in accident does not believe in God.

†

To adopt a purely moralistic attitude towards the evil which is in us and to strive to perfect ourselves by our own efforts is a superficial and absolutely fruitless occupation. If we gaze without God into the abyss of evil that is in us, our situation will appear hopeless to us. And if we hope to attain perfect virtue without God, this will make us fall into another trap—thinking ourselves equal to God.

In both cases there is a possible solution—the recognition of God's hand over us.

†

For all of us the way to Christ is this: the renunciation of our human nature, humility–'He must increase, but I must decrease' (John iii. 30)–to rejoice, hearing the voice of the Bridegroom. In our approach to Christ we cannot avoid the heroic self-negation of St. John the Baptist.

†

If we resolve always to obey the voice of conscience–for this is God's voice in us–such a resolution will develop in us the lost organ of communion with God.

†

It is clear why Cain and his posterity, Ham, and all the spiritual 'Hamites', are those who protest, who reject the law, who are enemies of the Godhead. The law of God is not their law, it is alien and even repulsive to them. On the contrary, the meek in spirit, 'the sons of Abel', see in the divine law something akin to them which they gladly and willingly obey, for they are 'sons of God'. Thus we willingly obey the traditions of *our* family, *our* school, the way of life of *our* people.

†

Cain and Abel (Esau and Jacob) are the ancestors of two human types: the 'Abelites', meek, passive, without initiative, and the 'Cainites', bellicose, active, inventive; the Slavs and the people of western Europe, in particular, are examples respectively of these two types.

†

'Hellenism' in the Holy Fathers—St. Gregory the Theologian: 'I have attained Athenian perfection' (Letter 128); he constantly quotes Homer, Pindar, the Stoics, Plato, recalls Athens.

†

Socrates is Orthodox in the structure of his soul: he has one of the essential traits of Orthodoxy—the hearts in 'earthen vessels' (2 Cor. iv. 7) illuminated by grace. It is precisely this that attracts us in Socrates.

†

Today, explaining the mysticism of Socrates, I found the following image. He made his interlocutors 'give birth' to their own thought. By his questions he created a highly rarified atmosphere around his interlocutor, destroying all the answers and decisions which the latter had taken over ready-made from other people. Eventually the person he was talking with felt like a mouse under the bell of a pneumatic pump; he was ideologically stifled, and with extreme effort and labour finally brought forth to birth into this emptiness his own original thought.

†

In the heuristic method of Socrates, humility and meekness are very striking. Instead of killing his adversary with one sharp blow, he has the patience of a mother, leading her child, picking it up many times and leading it on again and again.

†

All theological thought, all knowledge of the Church's teaching has no meaning—and, indeed, is impossible—if it does not come

142

from the fullness of a loving and believing heart. Then it is fruitful, meaningful, alive, and is the natural expression of a soul living in Christ.

†

After the Fall, man lost the capacity of knowing God, just as he lost the whole of himself. It was only the coming of the Saviour into this world that gave man the possibility of regaining his capacity of knowing God.

†

There are two forms of insensibility: the first is that of the naturally sensual man, replete, content; the second is the insensibility of a sinful, fallen man.

The first is unaware of the spiritual realm, the second has fallen away from it. The first has not grown sufficiently, the second has lost what he once had.

†

What a joy it is sometimes to behold in a soul the manifest effects of the working of faith, of the love of Christ.

Today, for instance: N's admission that after having experienced sorrow and turned to the Church for help, he feels entirely transfigured: what was a matter of routine, tedious, nearly dead, has been filled with a real, vivid content; the entire world begins to look different. Yes, experience, personal experience alone, can lead one to this grasp of the vitality and truth of the Church and of Christ's teaching. And, bitter though it is to admit it, suffering is the usual path that leads to this experience.

†

For people of our background, death is something unexpected, an absurdity; it does not harmonize or link up with any of the events that precede it. And because death is a phenomenon of the higher, divine order, this incompatibility points to an essential incompatibility between the whole order of our life and the divine order.

†

Death is always evil and terrifying, whether it is the death of an old man or a child, of a just man or a sinner. Death is always the victory of the devil, a temporary victory, yet a victory none the less. Our body, which was created for immortality, submits to the evil law of death, is separated from the soul, disrupted, stricken with decay, turned into nothing.

Through sin, death has entered the world; it enters into us from our very childhood, traces the wrinkles of sin on our faces, extinguishes the living fire in our eyes, disables our body. But Christ is the conqueror of sin and hell, and Christ's work is above all the victory over death through his Resurrection: 'If Christ be not risen . . . your faith is also vain' (1 Cor. xv. 14).

†

Hysteria is a disintegration of the personality; and it unleashes tremendous energies with a power for destruction as fatal as those of the split atom.

†

Our love for God already constitutes for us, in our own personal experience, the affirmation of His existence. Our love for God is God Himself within us; experiencing this love subjectively, we have already thereby acknowledged God.

This experience of love is the only path which is certain and self-evident. Before his heart has been moved in this manner, a man is deaf and blind towards everything, even towards a miracle. But once this feeling of God within himself has come to him, he needs miracles no longer: what has been accomplished within his own soul is a miracle in itself.

†

At Christ's entry into Jerusalem, when the enthusiastic crowds came out to meet him, there was a tragic hidden misunderstanding. Christ was going to voluntary suffering, while the crowds welcomed the beginning of His reign upon earth. The people were impressed by miracles, they had been fed by loaves, they wanted power and authority extended over them.

Christ could now do everything within the limits of 'this world', but the people who brought him adulation and honours did not bring him that which was essential—souls tempered by repentance, converted, transfigured.

In what spirit do we meet Christ? Do we not expect bread from Him, miracles on the material level, and do we not ourselves continue in our previous way of life, carnal and vain? But we have more than they, we have Golgotha, the Cross and the Resurrection of the Saviour, and this commits us to a different way of meeting Him.

Let us then bring to Him and place at His feet our contrition for the sin of our heart, our thirst for purification and for participation in 'the life of the age to come'.

†

Unfinished letter to N.

. . . If there exists in us even a faint inclination towards things spiritual, then, however deeply we are engrossed in a distracted

145

and busy life, we await with hope and trepidation the approach of the great days of repentance, and each time we hope to step a little higher on that mysterious ladder which lifts our hearts toward heaven.

The great and sad days of Lent are drawing near; after confession and communion, having cleansed our souls, having experienced tenderness and tears, conscious of new strength within us, we make the resolution to start a new way of life. But usually, on the very day on which we received Holy Communion, we stumble over trifles, hasten to amend our fault, make further blunders, more and then still more; finally, shrugging our shoulders, we sink for the entire year into our habitual and painless sinfulness. Then Lent approaches once again; at this very thought the 'inner man' awakes within us, hope lives again, and we await once more those blessed and saving days with trepidation and confidence, hoping for a final and secure restoration of our sluggish and sinful soul. But between these intentions and true contrition there stretches a long road, full of many obstacles, which is difficult to traverse. I do not speak of outward obstacles—the excess of business worries, thousands of external reasons: however great, these outward obstacles can be overcome, if we have an inner flame, a thirst for purification, and a sincere resolve to achieve it. Far more serious are the inner difficulties—lack of faith, passions, impurity and, last but not least, blindness concerning our sins and a 'petrified insensibility'—these two things in particular.

'To see your sins in all their multiplicity and hideousness—this is indeed a gift of God' (John of Kronstadt).

'He who knows his own sin is higher than the man who resurrects the dead by his prayers. He who has been granted the gift of seeing himself is superior to the man who has the gift of seeing angels' (St. Isaac the Syrian).

And vice versa—blindness to sin, the failure to see it, is the natural condition of fallen man. We unconsciously hide our sins from ourselves, our Lord himself puts part of our sins out of our view for a time, in order afterwards to throw us into terror and sorrow at the clear sight of the abyss of our impurity. But without a clear view of our sins there is no repentance; and if there is no repentance, there is no salvation. 'Let me behold my sins': such is the natural, prayerful sigh of each of us who enters the great season of Lent. To do so, we must not spare ourselves but must renounce ourselves and all our sinful nature. . . .

†

'The sweetness of this world': every time we plunge into blind, carnal delight we destroy the spiritual life. Why? Because we lose spiritual sobriety, clarity of thought, self-control; our attention is distracted, our will is weakened, our personality is enfeebled, dissolved, and dissipated. Asceticism demands a renunciation of all that is pleasant—in food, clothes, bedding, relations with people, and so on. There must be a sublimation, a transition to higher values.

†

Earthly happiness—love, family, youth, health, enjoyment of life and nature—all this is good, and we must not think that Christianity severely condemns it all.

What is bad is *enslavement* to our happiness, so that this happiness possesses us and we are entirely engrossed in it, forgetting what is essential.

And from the point of view of spiritual growth, sufferings are to be valued, not in themselves but only according to their results. Depriving man of earthly happiness, they place him face to face with the highest values, forcing him to open his eyes to himself and the world, turning him towards God.

Thus an earthly happiness combined with the constant remembrance of God, from which the tension of the spiritual life is not excluded, is indubitably a good thing. Similarly, if suffering irritates and humiliates a man without transfiguring him, without producing any salutary effects, it is doubly evil.

This is an answer to the very common conviction that the Church and the Gospels condemn *all* earthly happiness and invite us to suffer for the sake of suffering.

†

. . . I enjoy the quiet here,[1] the freedom, and especially the complete leisure. This last is at times a definite necessity for the normal life of the soul. Our ordinary living, entirely absorbed as it is in business, and granting us scarcely a minute to breathe and collect ourselves, is seriously damaging to that subconscious life which must ripen in stillness and a certain apparent idleness.

†

I have a fixed dream of a hearth of my own—even, literally, of an open fireplace with its wood-fire, of books and a garden of my own. Of course these are vain dreams; our whole life, and the course of history itself, are opposed to this, leading as they do to the destruction of hearths, to the disintegration of family life, to the anthill and the beehive.

†

A fountain, and above it a crowned statue of the Virgin. The same image adorns my tiny room—a cheap statuette bought on the market place, but it has made me so happy. The peasant waters his horse by the fountain; other peasants, men and women, rake

---

[1] This and the following paragraphs were written while on holiday in the country.

hay. A silent, unhurried life; even the local train is in no hurry and carries only materials of good quality: logs, wood, pressed straw and hay; and the diabolical forces which rule the world cross this tiny, quiet human world only in the shape of motor-cars, flashing like lightning along the narrow strip of high-road covered with evil-smelling tar (as if to divide the world of devils from the world of God).

†

I have taken in advance the resolution never, except in extreme necessity, to live in a hotel. A hotel room, even in a good establishment, is full of alien emanations, harmful to my peace of mind. Alien smells, the bed on which thousands of other people have slept, the washstand with its inevitable wisp of someone else's hair—all this is disquieting, suspicious, false. How can one live and rest normally in such an environment? A private house is something entirely different, even if it is uncomfortable and inconvenient; everything in it is natural, human, agreeable.

†

We live in a farm-house between 250 and 300 years old: low ceilings with heavy beams, small windows, a chimney, fortress-like walls. In place of the original fireplace there is now an iron stove, but even this—especially on a wet day—gives a real sense of home, of cosiness, of something long desired. I think a real feeling of home can be had only by people who have lived in such nests as these, in houses of their own, with the real, living fire of a hearth and a smoky ceiling. What special attractions has our modern 'home' to offer?—a flat, one of a thousand all alike, with central heating, electric light, water-pipes instead of a well or fountain: a lodging devoid of all special characteristics, which can be easily exchanged for another. Thus modern civilization kills the sense of home, of family life, and opens the road to socialism, communism and anarchy, in men's souls as well as in outward life.

†

'Riding develops a feeling of freedom and power' (L. Brown). The horseman and horsemanship created knighthood and the entire culture of chivalry. What are the feelings stimulated by driving a car? What can chauffeurs bring to the world? What new culture will be created by the motor-car?

†

The home, the hearth, the penates. . . . In his excellent article, 'The Religious Sense of Pushkin', S. Frank[1] devotes a page to Pushkin's cult of the hearth, the penates, solitude.

It seems that Pushkin's poem: "'Tis time, my friend, 'tis time' was written on a sheet of paper which had on the back the inscription: 'How soon shall I transfer my penates to the country–to the fields, the garden, the peasants, to books, poetic work, family, love, religion, death.'

†

In what does the shame (and the shamelessness) of nakedness consist, and for what reason is there an injunction against it in the Bible and in the religious consciousness of peoples? I think that 'naked man' is the equivalent of 'sinful man', a man fallen away from God's glory. The bodies of our forefathers and of the saints are clothed 'with light, as with a garment' (Psalm civ. 2); for us who have fallen, the light is replaced by clothes until the times

---

[1] Simeon Frank (1877–1950), Russian philosopher and religious writer.

shall be fulfilled. The 'state of nakedness' represents our defiance of God, our self-affirmation in sin.

†

Today, as I watched a young peasant worker on the tram platform, I thought: how little space does the face occupy in a man's entire figure, and how little space the eyes take up in his face; and I understood the words, 'the many-eyed cherubim'.

†

Good taste helps us to appreciate life, its harmony or discord, the relations between men; it assists us in ordering our life, our family, our home. Yet it sometimes makes us uncomfortable: we are offended by people's bad taste, where others would not have noticed anything. And these errors of taste are often committed by good and kind people, and we are prevented from becoming friends with them, we are made unkind.

If we could deepen this perception of ours, learning to see harmony and beauty (where they are to be found) beneath ugliness and disorder, we should be close to wisdom.

†

'The sun is an eternal window opening on the gold of dazzling light.' I seem to hear these words all the time, on this very hot day: sun, salt—*solntse, sol, sal.*[1] In ancient rituals the sun is symbolized by salt; the salt purified the sacrificial victim. The taste of the sun is bitter-salt, like that of the sea, and its odour reminds one of bitter herbs growing on dry rocks. Savory is much more a

---

[1] A play on words. *Sol* means 'sun' in Latin, 'salt' in Russian. (*Solntse* is the Russian for 'sun', *sal* the Latin for 'salt'.)

sun plant than are dewy roses. These were my thoughts as, sitting on a tombstone, I rubbed a spray of wormwood between my fingers and smelled it.

†

Here I am in the place where I am to rest.[1] It is impossible not to recuperate here—the sun, the air, the abundance of mountain torrents, the smell of the woods and of the distant meadows, rising from below.

I also like the lowlands, the valleys, but infinitely less and in a different way—probably just as people like sin, I like the warmth, 'the abundance of the fruits of the earth'.[2] But here there is ascetic bareness.

I wanted to find a road leading to the naked ridge which rises above the woods. Today, I was on that ridge. It's a two mile climb and I came up to the summit along a winding path: the whole of Savoie lay before me with her peaks and ridges.

And at my feet, among the meadows, I noticed—flooded with sunshine and surrounded by sparse pine-trees—ruined foundations, heaps of stones. They immediately struck me as somewhat mysterious. Later I learned that these are the remains of a Roman camp.

†

Today, I had a delightful walk. At first the ascent was rather dull—along an almost invisible path winding amidst chalk embankments through a forest of low, sparse pines. However, there were incidents to compensate for this: a hare sprang almost from under my feet; I wandered across barberry-bushes and sweet-briar, shedding its blossoms. I walked slowly, reading, as I went, the

---

[1] A remote village in the Savoie (south-east France).
[2] A phrase in the Litany of Peace at the beginning of the Liturgy.

Matins service and the Hours, sitting down to rest from time to time. I mounted the hill for about two hours and then reached the pass: immediately the whole landscape was transformed. To the left, a small village scattered round a church; to the right, lovely meadows; and, directly beyond the pass, an endless view opening on the mountains, streaked and spotted with snow. Around me and quite near to me—torn, craggy rocks. Below—green slopes of forest; and above all, an extraordinary, snow-saturated atmosphere and absolute silence. Only from below came the sound of the brook, and a hidden spring was babbling somewhere under a rock. I sat for a long time, enjoying the stillness, the mountains, the fragrance. At my side some immortelles were blooming, such as I have never seen before, blue with a heart of deep violet. In the valley below there were no flowers at all, but here on the hillside they were as abundant as if they had sprung, not from the earth, but from the air and sun. And I thought: this is why mountains are so beautiful; through them, as through a friendship with some wise human being, one drinks in freshness, clarity, calm—the qualities born of high altitudes.

†

During this trip I have greatly appreciated the severe beauty of Corsica; most characteristic of this island are the grey granite rocks and impenetrable clusters of bushes, the famous *maquis*. A few trees along the road—eucalyptus and olive; this lends to the landscape a very complex design, dry and sharply outlined. And then there is the sea which is in sight all the time, stretching as far as the horizon, lying at your feet and curving inwards in bays, divided by long banks of rock running far out to sea. These banks are surmounted by round towers, where beacons were formerly lighted to serve as danger signals.

After three days of continual driving around the island (baptisms of children born quite a while ago, and memorial services for Russians long dead), I spent a truly wonderful day. I got up as the sun was rising. I went to the sea along the dusty road. On both sides of the road ran thick stone walls (behind which, in fiction and in reality, the local people pursue their vendettas). Then, crossing the fields overgrown with wormwood, I made my way down to the beach. Pinkish sand with grains as large as buck-wheat; the quiet bay with its crystal-clear waters delicately lapping the shore; the white lighthouse perfectly reflected in the bay. Not a soul around. The air was still cool, and so the water seemed quite warm to me.

And here is the thought which came to my mind as I was sun-bathing on the sand, wearing my bathing suit: I did not feel at all like a priest. How much dress means! And yet, I hardly ever have the feeling of not being a priest. I almost always feel like one and am relaxed and satisfied; if by chance I lose this sense, as I did just now, I always rebuke myself.

Generally speaking, I am very pleased that I took this trip. I did not expect to find anything which could move or surprise me so much. The Riviera scarcely appeals to me, but Corsica appears familiar and real. Is it her desert-like landscapes, her wildness and austerity, the granite rocks, the strong aroma of herbs and bushes? Perhaps, her resemblance with the landscapes of Palestine and Sinai? In any case I will leave a little bit of my heart here.

†

Today I stayed a long while on the *Pierre Plate*. It was very pleasant—a calm, blue day. I sunbathed, listened to the bells ringing far away in the valley and experienced at times an unusual feeling: 'I taste a sense of quiet that is new to my soul.' And indeed, the quiet is extraordinary—quiet all around me, quiet that enters my soul. I stayed there till sunset. At first, the valleys seemed to fill with pink dust, while the distant mountains were still bathed in sunshine. Then the light faded and they turned to mauve, while the valleys were tinged with blue. Autumn is already apparent, there are hardly any flowers left, the grass has been cropped short by the goats, and the leaves have turned a paler colour, though none are yellow as yet.

†

It is still pleasant here, perhaps better than in summer. From early morning, there is a clearness of air and a brightness of sky. An amazing quiet, the quiet of the mountains. It is very warm, even hot in the sun, but there is a touch of autumn in the shade. Sometimes, at about two o'clock, clouds gather right overhead. But in the evening the sky is completely clear once more. In spite of this I still feel all the time somehow embarrassed without a church, as if I had been placed in a false position. This prevents me from enjoying my rest completely. I have realized here even more clearly that a priest should not leave his church even for a single day.

†

In Cannes, yesterday, I performed my first baptism. I was very tired after the evening service, because of officiating for the first time without a deacon. Several times I felt quite faint; it was very painful. But when I saw the tiny, fourteen days old girl, the parents, the baptismal font gilded and lit up by the three candles, I was so deeply moved (I did not expect this) that all my fatigue vanished. I performed the baptism with great inspiration, emotion and joy. Valentina X is my first godchild. Glory be to Thee, O God.

†

The usual feeling experienced when giving a sermon, especially in front of people brought together by mere chance (in the religious sense), is that one is speaking to unbelievers; and so all the words about Christ, faith, miracles, are transformed into a tacit, mutually understood lie. I am speaking to people who are presumed to be believers, though I know that this is not true of most of them. For their part they think: 'You are obliged to preach because it is part of your job, and I must listen to you for decency's sake without betraying too much of my boredom.' That is why I often say nothing. It is very easy to talk to the sick, the aged, the poor, for instance in hospitals and veterans' homes.

†

In sleep, when our normal consciousness fades away and we lose our self-control, when we are entirely sincere and ashamed of nothing—then there rises from the depth of the sub-conscious the primary basis of our being, the deepest strata of our soul are uncovered, and we appear then, as at no other time, in our own true selves. The images, visions, and states of our soul most typical of our dreams, are the truest, undisguised manifestation of our real personality.

Of course, we must here distinguish purely psychic phenomena (such as prayers and chants after prolonged religious services) as well as what is merely the effect of our physical condition, to which we are so closely subject (for instance, nightmares caused by the liver). But assuming an objective and skilled power of judgement, the character and content of our dreams can help us considerably to know ourselves, opening our eyes to more than one aspect of ourselves.

†

No matter how fashions change, women's mourning attire

remains the same: when in grief, a woman does not invent but takes the ready-made, the generally accepted. In this we find the explanation of all conservatism; whatever is serious is conservative. The most conservative manifestation in human life is religion, because it is the deepest one. Reform starts when the soul is empty (I speak of change in *forms*); therefore revolution is always a sign that the spiritual life of a nation has become impoverished.

†

Our continual mistake is that we do not concentrate upon the present day, the actual hour, of our life; we live in the past or in the future; we are continually expecting the coming of some special moment when our life will unfold itself in its full significance. And we do not notice that life is flowing like water through our fingers, sifting like precious grain from a loosely fastened bag.

Constantly, each day, each hour, God is sending us people, circumstances, tasks, which should mark the beginning of our renewal; yet we pay them no attention, and thus continually we resist God's will for us. Indeed, how can God help us? Only by sending us in our daily life certain people, and certain coincidences of circumstance. If we accepted every hour of our life as the hour of God's will for us, as the decisive, most important, unique hour of our life—what sources of joy, love, strength, as yet hidden from us, would spring from the depths of our soul!

Let us then be serious in our attitude towards each person we meet in our life, towards every opportunity of performing a good deed; be sure that you will then fulfil God's will for you in these very circumstances, on that very day, in that very hour.

†

If we loved God better, how easily we would entrust to Him ourselves and the whole world with all its contradictions and riddles. All men's difficulties are caused by their lack of love towards each other. Where there is love, there can be no difficulties.

Many perplexities experienced by the Christians of our days would be solved, if we were truly Christians in the direct, evangelical sense of the word. We would thus solve among other questions that of the meaning of suffering 'as our Lord suffers', and many others. Given our greedy, blind attachment to earthly goods, —which in itself creates great suffering—how can we speak of the *religious* meaning of our life and of our suffering?

†

How can we strengthen our life in the Church?

The direction of a spiritual father, continual contact with him.

Frequent resort to the sacraments, careful preparation before receiving them, participation in Church services, prayer at home, the daily reading of the Gospel and religious books, the observance of the Church calendar, friendship and contact with people who believe and belong to the Church.

†

Here is our task: having renounced ourselves, to remain ourselves, to realize God's plan for us.

†

The approach of light is terrifying, torturing to darkness and sin. I constantly observe that people stubbornly avoid Holy Communion. They go to church as if carried there by an inner impulse, then stand outside in the courtyard. Many have admitted as much to me.

†

Between spiritual growth and garrulousness there is an inverse ratio. The substitution of loquacity for spiritual tension is easy and attractive. It is a temptation for all who teach.

†

In the morning and evening prayers: 'Have mercy on *me*' . . . 'purify *me*' . . . '*I* shall open *my* mouth' and so on . . .: 'I' before God.

In the Lord's prayer: '*Our* Father' . . . '*our* daily bread' . . . 'forgive *us*' . . . and in the Liturgy: 'Holy God, have mercy on *us*.' Two modes of feeling: personal (of the Desert Fathers) and ecclesial.

†

'I have a deep faith', is a platitude on the lips of all conceited, limited people who are weak in faith. The Apostles, though they saw Christ with their own eyes and touched Him, still prayed: 'Increase our faith.' The Gospels state with precision the marks of profound faith: 'And these signs shall follow them that believe: In my name shall they cast out devils . . . they shall lay hands on the sick, and they shall recover' (Mark xvi. 17–18). 'Nothing shall be impossible unto you' (Matt. xvii. 20). 'And all things, whatsoever ye shall ask in prayer, believing, ye shall receive' (Matt. xxi. 22). Does this sound like us? We, who are so cold, powerless, spiritually weak?

†

In the parable of the prodigal son we have a long story about the path of the human soul which has fallen away from the Father's house, sunk to the lowest depths, and risen again through repentance. Every single word in the story, every image provides us with material for lengthy reflection: separation from the Father as the beginning of sin, the journey to a far-away land, squandering of riches, and all the other symbols of the parable. Let us pause at the crucial point of the story, let us consider how the sinner first began to rise from the abyss, how this miracle was accomplished.

The prodigal son, having claimed his own share of the inheritance, lost everything in this world and was deprived of all the joys of life; he lost his fatherland, his family's support; he did not have a piece of bread left and was entirely alone: all the roads of this world were closed to him. 'Tribulation and anguish, upon every soul of man that doeth evil' (Rom. ii. 9). And it is at this point that the divine miracle is performed—in the very confinement there is liberation; in the very grief, salvation. Among us too there are people who have reached the limits of grief. It seems to them that destruction is all around them—let them be comforted. When man reaches this point when all roads are closed to him horizontally, then the road *upwards* opens before him. If compressed on all sides, water rises; so the soul, compressed, imprisoned, walled in by grief, rises to heaven. We are fortunate if we detach ourselves inwardly, in time and on our own initiative, from the broad way of worldliness, if neither the comforts of life, nor riches, nor success, fill our hearts and lead us away from that which is essential.

Otherwise, God in His wrath shatters our idols—our comfort, our career, our health, our family—in order that we may understand at last that there is but one God before whom we must bow in worship.

But, it might be objected, do we not find that in many cases suffering, so far from bringing man back to God, bears no fruit, but crushes him and is therefore meaningless?

Turn to the prodigal son of the parable. Why were his sufferings salutary? Why, when he 'came to himself', did he discover the path of salvation? Because he remembered his Father's house, because he was firmly convinced that such a house does really exist, because he loved it, because—and let us here discard the language of symbolism—that sinner *believed* in God.

This is the saving power of suffering. This is what opens the gates of God's house—the only gates at which it is worth knocking.

†

Tears are of such great value, because they shake our entire organism. In tears and sufferings our earthly flesh thaws and a spiritual body, angelic flesh, is born.

The spiritual body is created through tears, fasting, vigils.

†

What are sleepiness, absent-mindedness, difficulty in prayer, 'petrified insensibility', if not obvious death, the result of sin which is killing us, a death before death, revealed to us in the form of direct experience and self-observation?

Who will restore and revive us? What power can bring to life that which is dead? The power of God: and we place our faith in it again and again.

†

In this life we know *for certain* one thing only: that we shall die. This is the only fixed, inevitable fact common to all men. Everything else is changing, unstable, corruptible. If we love the world, its joy and beauty, we must also make room in our life for this last, final moment—our death; for if we wish it to be so, this too can be beautiful.

†

Self-knowledge, introspection into the depth of our soul, are important in order to make clear precisely where our weak points lie. There ensues a struggle against the darkness in our souls, so that we may approach the light consciously. Just as there are bodily ailments, in the same way each of us suffers from his own spiritual ailments, with their distinctive peculiarities; just as there is a specific bodily cure for each illness and for each human being, in the same way—besides a 'spiritual régime' common to all of us—we must each pursue our own struggle, a struggle directed specifically against the sins and vices inherent in us personally.

†

It is not only sin that is terrifying, but also the despair and defection bred by sin. Isaac the Syrian has this to say concerning such a condition: 'Have no fear, even though you fall daily; do not abandon prayer; stand up courageously, and the angel who watches over you will honour your patience.' Let us recall the words of Christ in such cases: 'Go and sin no more.' And that is all: no curses, no excommunications. We must not submit to the evil spirit of dejection that seeks to draw us ever deeper into sin. Again and again, we must fall at Christ's feet, again and again He will accept us.

†

I gain a great deal from reading Isaac the Syrian. In particular, the spirit diffused throughout his writings is excellent—tender wisdom and love, the deepest compassion for sinful humanity; his remarkable style, the terseness and force of his sayings. How convincing he is when he says that, since we have been driven out of paradise with thorns and thistles as our portion, we must not be surprised if we have to sow and harvest among thorns, and if we are badly pricked by them, even when our intentions are of the best and we are acting righteously. All this must continue until we find in our heart the paradise of divine love; and then, even here upon earth, everything will become joyous and radiant for us. Let God send us but the foretaste of this joy, and we shall live and work meanwhile without murmuring, even though it be among 'thorns'.

†

All resistance to God has a base origin. Genuine spiritual nobility consists in submission to the Supreme Being.

†

In all life, including the Christian life, wisdom consists in this: not to be exacting towards people.

†

Some do not give alms, saying: it will be spent on drink, and so forth. Even if it is spent on drink, the sin is less serious than the anger we provoke by our refusal, and the harshness and condemnation which we cultivate in ourselves.

†

We know little, and in most cases do not try to find out anything about our church services, about the life of the Church. We should fill this gap and become living members of the Church. Few people even realize that the so-called 'choir' speaks and sings in the name of the entire congregation, and that in the early Church there were none of those specially trained, professional singers who now perform this 'duty'. All sang, testifying *their own* faith and with a sense of responsibility for the words they uttered. Sometimes we do not even know the words. And how many understand them? When we attend a service in church, we seem to sign a letter we have not read, to assume duties which we ignore. The Church is alive and will live for ever. Let us not hang like dry, withered leaves on this ever-living tree.

†

I observe in people a certain peculiarity from which I infer what seems to me an important psychological law. Often those who have quite enough time at their disposal are nevertheless late in their words and actions. There is in them a certain resistance of which they are hardly conscious, a resistance to *any* sort of action, whether agreeable or disagreeable or indifferent. When it comes to saying, undertaking, or doing something, they unconsciously put on the brakes, performing a number of small, unnecessary acts, so as to defer the task which stands before them; and therefore they are always late. I think this mechanism can be discovered in every soul; in some cases it amounts to a psychotic condition; in sanctity it disappears. Here we have a kind of elementary type of sin, a 'clean' sin, disinterested and purposeless.

†

A conceited man is hopelessly blind and solitary; in the world and in human beings he sees nothing but himself.

†

164

Since the beginning of the world men have died; since the beginning of the world it has been well enough known that all earthly things are unstable, fleeting, corruptible. And yet, with a sort of blind greed, men stake all they possess, all the forces of their souls, upon this card which is bound to be trumped. They take their wealth to a bank which will certainly become insolvent.

†

There is one solid asset to the credit of our times: the conviction that there is no happiness to be found in the way of the world, in the path of personal gain. Until now, the whole life of this world was directed towards the goal of personal earthly happiness. Now this goal has been taken away from humanity. We all know that in these uncertain, treacherous times, no efforts will suffice to build this house of cards which constitutes our personal happiness. This represents one of the deepest sources of instability in our day. The world wavers like the two scales of a balance. 'We dare not recognize the power of the Beast, nor the light yoke of Christ.'

What is the task of the Christian in such critical times? Our choice is made, we have willingly accepted the 'light yoke of Christ'. In this struggle between the forces of light and of darkness, we must surrender all our energies, capacities, talents and material resources to the power of good, and we shall then inherit the things which Christ promised in the Beatitudes to those who follow in His path, and not in the treacherous ways of earthly happiness.

†

The affirmation that we are made after the image and likeness of God is our measure, our conscience, the path which we must follow. All other paths lead to a loss of ourselves, to the deforming of our personality; there is only one true path for man—

transfiguration into the image of God, return to the state which was ours when we were created, but which we have since disfigured.

†

The world is a system of symbols *a realibus ad realiora.*[1] The spiritual world is reflected in the corporeal forms of this world – 'the example and shadow of heavenly things' (Hebr. viii. 5). The value of symbols lies in the joy springing from the knowledge that our world is a likeness of that other world. Hence the significance of icons, candles, smoke of incense.

†

Is the whole universe corrupted by the fall of man? Do we not contemplate paradisial worlds when looking at the stars?

†

Despite all, the soul seeks happiness. Sorrow, suffering, are not in themselves characteristic of man. Is not this instinctive turning to joy and light the soul's memory of paradise lost, and its striving towards it?

†

The so-called baseness of our flesh, its inherent sinfulness – such notions are deeply mistaken. The flesh is sinful in so far as the soul is sinful. Although tainted with sin, it is *sacred* and is, in its essence, the image of God.

According to God's original plan, the body was sacred, and the soul within it sacred. The fall of man and the punishment incurred by sin involved both the soul and the body at the same

---

[1] *A realibus ad realiora*, 'from reality to a higher reality': a formula of religious symbolism employed by the Russian poet Vyacheslav Ivanov (1886–1949).

time. And we must purify our body as well as our soul. 'I am the image of Thine ineffable glory, even though I bear the wounds of sin.' We must apply treatment to these wounds and so bring back once more that beauty which once was ours—'a beauty after the image and likeness of God', which will arise from the dead and participate in the glory of God.[1]

†

All the virtues are nothing without humility: take, for example, the Pharisees. To possess all the virtues, except humility, is like being shipwrecked as you enter port. The characteristics of humility: not to believe in our own merits, not to be so much as aware of them (meekness), not to judge, to rejoice at being humiliated. And through humility we enter at once upon the blessings promised in the Beatitudes.

†

Only now do we realize the fatal lack of understanding displayed towards the Russian national spirit: as a result, men thought that they were guarding Russia but actually destroyed her. This mistaken method of defence led to the persecution of the Slavophiles and to the absurd and brutal harrying of the 'Old Believers', the burning of their icons, the sealing of their churches, the destruction of their sanctuaries and altars—in other words, to the oppression of the most faithful champions of the Russian spirit.

†

The ancient style of icon-painting corresponds to ancient piety (prayer, the perception of God, and so on). This, so it seems,

---

[1] Father Alexander is quoting here from hymns used at the Orthodox funeral service.

is why we have failed in our attempt to master the ancient style, for the form of our piety does not coincide with that which prevailed between the eleventh and the sixteenth centuries. New ventures must spring from the fullness of a new spiritual life; otherwise we shall obtain nothing genuine. Nevertheless, in so far as we are in some way leading a true spiritual life and life of prayer, it will follow the eternal pattern, such as we find in St. Paul, in Symeon the New Theologian.[1] Therefore an icon painted according to the ancient rules, even a modest copy, serves the same purpose as the reading of the ancient ascetics—it helps us to strengthen the weakness of our spiritual life.

†

Realistic painting represents a sinful perception of the world. Therefore the decoration of churches in the realistic 'Italian' style wounds our religious feeling. An icon painted according to the 'canon' is at the opposte extreme to this sinful perception: in such icons we have a world transfigured, all is ordered according to ritual and is full of beauty.

†

Modern atheists, denying religion, struggling against it, cannot however remain entirely without religion, for the cult of the Absolute is implanted in the nature of man. And so they involuntarily create a pitiful imitation of religion, the cult of leaders (saints), even of their remains (relics), religious devotion to their doctrine (the Gospels), and so on—replacing the eternal and the beautiful by their own mediocre and temporal cult; and yet, even the latter springs from that very same need, which they cannot stifle in themselves. But the substitution of a false for the true

---

[1] St. Symeon the New Theologian (949–1022), abbot of the monastery of St. Mamas in Constantinople, Byzantine mystical writer.

faith leads them into a spiritual confusion: while the religious need seems outwardly to be satisfied, their religion does not really feed the spirit.

†

Rationalism and materialism, denying religion, seeking to explain scientifically all the secrets of creation, display first of all scientific dishonesty, for in fact they do not explain anything, they do not give any positive answer to many questions, and refuse to admit their own bankruptcy. Their fundamental error lies in the fact that they do not see that human reason is crippled by sin–this very human reason, which forms the basis of their whole construction. Their second mistake is this, that they think everything can be explained; hence their pitiful and fruitless attempts to give a materialistic explanation of everything, whereas the very essence of religion lies in recognition that human nature is corrupted by sin, and consequently reason is corrupted as well: that is why it must submit itself to the Absolute and recognize the existence of a mystery. Religion does not seek to explain everything, because here on earth there is no complete explanation; but it gives a promise and a foretaste of a harmony that exists in the other world, where all contradictions will be resolved.

†

There are various forms of spiritual blindness; one is that of the people who err sincerely, through lack of knowledge (Saul, the heathens); another, that of men steeped in sin, stupefied by passion; another still, the blindness of those who have lost the criteria of truth, of the proud (my opinion is the truth, what I do not hold is error). In order that some of these souls should regain their sight, it is only necessary that they should be presented with the truth; for others, the remedy is repentance. 'With the eyes of my soul blinded, I come to Thee, O Christ, as the man blind from birth, crying to Thee in repentance: Thou art the dazzling Light of those in darkness' (Kontakion for the fifth Sunday after Easter).

†

How often we are blind, not seeing our own sins; blind, when we see the faults of other people (or fail to see other people's good qualities); blind, when we think that we possess the truth and reject the point of view of others. May God send us wise simplicity, may He restore the sight of our eyes, blinded by the darkness of sin, so that we may see ourselves and the entire world in the light of Christ's truth.

†

Why is our love of God weak? Because our faith is weak. And our faith is weak because we are indifferent to the things of God. Through the study and knowledge of these things faith will arise, and from faith will come love.

†

To know something is to go out of oneself and to enter into communion with the thing that is known.

Knowledge of truth is communion with Truth. To strive towards the knowledge of God is to touch His glory, life in God. To know God is to become like Him.

†

It is impossible to remain for ever in a state of spiritual exaltation. God allows certain intermissions in our fervour because He does not wish either to deprive us of the courage by which we climb higher, or to feed the pride which leads us to fall. Let our heart advance on the path along which God leads us.

True, these alternations are a painful trial; but it is good for us to know from our own experience that our moments of spiritual exaltation do not depend upon us, but are the gift of God which He takes away when He deems it necessary.

If we always retained this gift of God, we should feel neither the weight of the cross nor our own powerlessness. Our trials would not be real trials, our good actions would be valueless.

Let us therefore patiently bear the periods of depression and of aridity of the heart. They teach us humility and the distrust of ourselves. They make us feel how unstable and weak is our spiritual life, they make us turn more often to divine help.

In this state of unfeeling dryness of the heart, in the absence of fervent prayer we must be careful not to give up our spiritual exercises, our daily prayers. If we abandoned them, we should do ourselves the greatest damage.

We are inclined to think that if we do not feel definite satisfaction in prayer, it is not worth while praying.

In order to realize how wrong we are in thinking this, it is enough to remember that prayer and the love of God are one and the same. The essence of prayer does not just consist in those feelings of joy which sometimes accompany it. Loving prayer may sometimes exist without such feelings; and this is a more purified and disinterested form of prayer, since, being deprived of spiritual joy, its goal is God alone.

We may feel deprived of blessed consolations and yet preserve a firm will, submitting to all the difficulties which God sends us, and humbly accepting everything, even the sense of spiritual depression which we experience.

If we succeed in enduring our periods of dryness of the heart in such a way as this, we shall find that they are a salutary spiritual exercise.

†

To pray fervently is a gift from God. To pray as well as we can is something that lies within our own power. So let us send up to God this weak, insufficient, dry prayer, as the only prayer that we are capable of offering, like the widow's mite in the Gospel. Then 'God's strength will flood your helplessness; and the prayer that is dry and distracted but frequent and resolute, having become a habit, having grown to be your second nature, will turn into a prayer that is meritorious, luminous, and full of fire' (Mark the Ascetic).[1]

†

People keep saying, 'Life is hard!' And if you cite the examples of the saints, the usual reply is: 'Well, they are not saints for nothing, it is easy for them!' A common error. It is the saints in particular who found it hard. They overcame not only worldly difficulties but the very essence of their humanity. The usual path of the saint—from the abyss of sin to the summit of holiness—is narrow and arduous. Whereas our course is always an easy one, along the line of least resistance; but the *fruits* of our course are bitter and burdensome, whereas the hard way yields the reward of true beatitude.

†

There are three degrees of obedience: to ask advice when we feel wholly perplexed; to follow a counsel which agrees with our

---

[1] Greek monastic writer of the fifth century.

own thoughts and inclinations, with our point of view; and finally to obey, even in direct opposition to our own views and wishes. This last alone is true obedience.

†

If we are not allowed to judge, how can we help our erring brother? By turning our attention to the beam in our own eye; only then, after we have struggled to remove it, shall we understand how deep-seated are the causes of sin, how hard it is to fight against it, what are the means whereby it can be cured, how great are the pity and compassion that the sinner deserves; and these feelings of ours, and our experience of the struggle with sin, will help us to remove the more from our brother's eye – through compassion, example, love. Judgement will disappear of itself.

†

'The desert lulls the passions to sleep', but man is still required to uproot them (Isaac the Syrian). This is the advantage of living in the world: through our meetings and conflicts with people and circumstances, such a life reveals our passions and sinful inclinations to us.

†

An ambitious man is like a common bit of glass, glistening and gay in rays of light; and the stronger the light, the more the glass sparkles; but in the absence of light it is dull and colourless.

†

How great is the strength of humility, and how helpless we are without it. If we sense the faintest tinge of self-righteousness in a preacher or speaker, this not only makes us blind to all his actual merits, but even arouses our antagonism. On the other hand, the humble man, even if he possesses no great intelligence or talent, conquers all hearts (Curé d'Ars).[1]

†

The essence of pride is to shut yourself off from God. The essence of humility is to let God inhabit you.

Through the sin of pride into which one man fell, all humanity, sharing his nature, fell also; and through the humility of one woman who was 'of our race', the whole of humanity was reborn.

†

All our life is taken up with judging others. We do not spare their good name; wantonly, sometimes even with no evil intention, we judge and slander—often through mere force of habit. Just as autumn leaves rustle, fall and rot, poisoning the air, even so censoriousness destroys everything we do, creating an atmosphere of distrust and anger, causing the perdition of our soul.

The signs of unjustified judgement: partiality, anger, lack of love, resulting from over-indulgence towards ourselves, blindness towards our own sinfulness, and exaggerated demands upon others.

We cease to judge others the moment we remember our infinite indebtedness towards God. Our lack of charity, our inexorability and mercilessness towards our fellow men, raise a barrier between ourselves and God's mercy, estranging us from Him.

†

Let us be more loving, more indulgent towards each other—we

---

[1] Jean-Baptiste Vianney (1786–1859), parish priest in France near Lyons, canonized in 1905.

are all so much in need of mutual love and help, and all our difficulties and sorrows are so insignificant in the face of eternity.

†

How is it that men have failed to notice that practically nothing has ever been achieved through hostility and anger, while meekness and gentleness always achieve everything? I mean, of course, achievements in the moral and spiritual realm, but I am convinced that this is also a more reliable way in the realm of ordinary life.

†

Our self-knowledge is amazingly superficial. By self-knowledge I do not, of course, mean a gnawing self-analysis, nor a morbid self-flagellation, nor that concentration on ourselves which has its source in pride. I mean an attentive, calm survey of the soul, a gaze turned inward, a deliberate effort to build up our lives consciously, so that we are not carried away by every passing emotion and idea. We are not in the slightest degree our own masters. We need practice, the discipline of attentive and determined work upon ourselves.

†

The centurion in the Gospel (Matt. viii) is the image of the perfect man: 'having soldiers under him, he says to this man, Go (to evil thoughts), and he goeth, and to another, Come (to the good in him) and he cometh, and to his servant (to his body), Do this, and he doeth it' (Matt. viii. 9).

We find the contrary where the average man is concerned—absentmindedness, disharmony, undisciplined feelings and will; and we should note that only return to faith and to the Church brings order out of this chaos of the soul, enabling it to share in the harmony that springs from these things.

†

We must not 'measure' ourselves.

†

Coercion, even for a good end, invariably provokes resistance and irritation. The only way to convince a man is to furnish him with an example such as will inspire him with the desire to embark on the same course: then, and then alone, will conversion be complete and fruitful, since only then will it be a free and independent act.

†

Obedience does not kill, it strengthens a man's spiritual will.

†

The virtue of gratitude, like all our other virtues, like fervent prayer and fasting, is first of all necessary for our own selves. The presence within us of a feeling of gratitude proves by itself that we are really imbued with an unflinching faith and love of God. Our gratitude is evidence of a correctly ordered religious soul.

We all know how to ask; even unbelievers turn to God in an emergency; but we do not know how to thank. A prayer of thanksgiving is the sign of an exalted soul. It is good to remember God in the day of misfortune; but not to forget Him in the day of happiness—this is the mark of a soul firmly rooted in God. A prayer of petition can exist in our heart with egoism, pride, anger; a prayer of thanksgiving is incompatible with such feelings.

Let us then appeal to God in our misfortunes and difficulties, but let us strive to advance to a higher stage—that of thanksgiving.

†

Typical 'stumbling blocks':

1. 'All men are egoists, all deeds are egoistic, even when they seem good and unselfish: for everyone who performs a good action obtains satisfaction and pleasure from it.'

If I get satisfaction from a good deed, this is an unforeseen and unexpected result, and it does not mean that I do good in order to obtain this satisfaction. There are many impulses and actions totally devoid of selfishness—performed, that is to say, without any calculated desire to receive a reward; in such cases, a person would hardly refuse to perform the good deed, just because he knows beforehand that it will bring him nothing.

2. 'The saints are egoists, they think only of their salvation.'

This is not true. Saints are people who are attracted by the Divine. Can you find fault with a plant because it is attracted to the light?

3. 'Asceticism is useless. My body does not trouble me, therefore I need not struggle against it. The main thing is to love God and my neighbour, whereas asceticism is an unnecessary preoccupation with onself.'

If the body hindered St. Seraphim, the Buddha, and even Christ, why then does it not hinder you? It is because you do not know yourself nor your sins, you are not conscious of any spiritual goal, towards which you direct your efforts. In order to love God and your neighbour, you must have a feeling for them and be refined by asceticism.

Asceticism is necessary first of all for creative action (of any kind), for prayer, for love: in other words, it is needed by every man throughout his entire life.

4. 'Why does God fail to relieve our sufferings?'

The greatest sufferings are those caused by sinful anger, self love, jealousy, the desire for revenge; every sin results in pain and grief ('tribulation and anguish, upon every soul of man that doeth evil', Rom. ii. 9). Is God to blame for these sufferings? Do we wish that sin should not bring suffering, that there should be no need to atone for sin, that the world should be drowned in sin? 'Our sins burn us and are consumed by grief.'

†

Do not be in a hurry to fill up an empty space with words and embellishments, before it has been filled with a deep interior content.

†

It is human to love those who love us and to hate those who hate us. There are two opposite ways in which we can depart from this attitude: God's way—to love those who hate; and the devil's way—to hate and insult those who love.

†

How shall we distinguish good from evil in actions and in men? The only measure is the feeling of joy, peace, love; and, conversely, the feeling of doubt and confusion. Here we find a means of almost unerring judgement.

†

Why are childhood impressions so important? Why is it essential to fill a child's mind and soul with light and goodness, starting from the very earliest stages of its life? In childhood we find a natural gift for faith, simplicity, gentleness, a capacity for tenderness, compassion, imagination, an absence of cruelty and hardness. Now this is precisely the kind of soil that yields a harvest thirty-fold, sixtyfold, or an hundredfold. When, later in life, the soul has become hard and dry, a man can be cleansed anew and saved by the continuing presence of his childhood experience. That is why it is so important to keep children close to the Church—it will provide them with nourishment for their entire lifetime.

†

Contact with children teaches us sincerity, simplicity, the ability to live in the present hour, the present action—an essential element in Orthodoxy.

Children are, in a sense, reborn daily: hence their spontaneity, the lack of complexity in their souls, the simplicity of their judgements and actions.

Moreover, their intuitive distinctions between good and evil are direct and straightforward, their souls are free of the bonds of sin, they are not continually judging and analysing.

All this we possess as a birthright which we wantonly scatter on our way, so that afterwards we must painfully gather up the fragments of our lost fortune.

†

I would like to write a work devoted to the *seven deadly sins*. The characteristics of each sin, a general picture of it, its varieties, causes, sources and interconnections, its symptoms, the means of struggling against it. Its marks in cases which are complicated. I think such a work would be useful to those who seek true repentance.

†

Last night, when I remained alone on the hill, the wind was so strong and it was so cold that I locked the door and the windows, and for the first time I slept at night with the windows closed. It was a little sad. Here is the test of our inner riches: have you enough to live on inwardly, if you are cut off from outside impressions, deprived of contact with people, of sensations of sight and hearing, and plunged into complete solitude? I thought of this with terror.

Here I have books, my favourite work, the opportunity of going out to look at nature—and yet, I feel sad from time to time. True, it rains almost all day long, the grass is never dry. All the same, I took an hour's stroll in the woods, found some new paths, discovered a plantation of beautiful fir-trees, where the ground is entirely carpeted with deep moss; after the rain it looked particularly bright. I saw many mushrooms.

And today, from early morning, it's misty again and rainy. This sitting at home, scarcely ever going out, helped me to picture more vividly the way of life of the hermits observing silence in their solitary cells.

Solitude is an excellent experience and a valuable exercise. An experience: has your soul anything in reserve? Can you live inwardly, with everything exterior reduced to a minimum? For we live chiefly on outward impressions—people, business, worries. What would happen if we put all this aside? What if the doors of our exterior perception should be closed? The doors of the inner chamber of our soul would then grate open painfully and laboriously.

In the noises of the market in which we usually live, it is of course difficult even to suspect that these inner chambers exist in our souls. How much easier to pray in this solitude and sadness! The lamentations which the psalms offer up to God we feel as if they were our own.

†

The lives of many saints offer us instances of the salutary link between life in the desert and creativity in the wider sense.

†

In *The Brothers Karamazov* of Dostoevsky many kinds of philosophical fallacies are shown up, so that those who read the novel gain a sort of immunity against them.

The father, Fedor Pavlovich, is a deliberate atheist and egoist both in his principles and in actual life, in his moral standards and his everyday behaviour; his life is meaningless. As a contrast, the reader is given, not a theory, but an image of 'concrete sanctity'—his youngest son Alyosha.

The three brothers each offer an answer to life's purpose.

Dimitry is nature in the raw, with both its good and evil aspects —the purest naturalism. He shows us what happens to the natural man: he is not bad, he is even endowed with a feeling for goodness, a certain chivalry, love for God, and moral integrity—yet combined with these are all the opposite qualities. No physical strength, no wealth are of any value unless accompanied by moral and spiritual values. Dimitry is Chaos, pining for the Word which will give it shape. Hence his passion for theories, his awe before Ivan.

Dimitry is unreasoning life: Ivan is lifeless reason. Ivan despises life and loves death. A vast intelligence with nothing to live for; blind will, and a lifeless mind. His philosophy is atheistic idealism, and in his credo there are three main points:

(a) If there is no God, everything is permitted. But he knows that not everything is permitted: and so perhaps God does exist? His reason accepts God, but not his heart (a 'petrified heart').

(b) He does not accept the world: that is to say, the world exists, but he does not accept it, for it is wicked. He stands for life in the Old Testament period, in the period of law, not of mercy. But God's providence can be vindicated through a feeling for life, not on a rational plane.

(c) Ivan is willing to accept both God and the world, but he wants to correct them (the Legend of the Grand Inquisitor).

In contrast to Ivan, to his brother and his father, is presented the spiritual beauty of the Church. Not literally and formally, but in an image of sanctity, in the person of Ivan's brother Alyosha, who is the means whereby all the difficulties are resolved. Alyosha goes into the world, not to become like the world, but to make the world like the Church.

†

I have been swamped by a flood of celebrations, words of welcome, expressions of good will.[1] On the one hand, they smother me with compliments and praise which they openly express, on the other hand, they stuff me with dinners; the one and the other between them kill all that is good in the soul. I sometimes feel completely drained and exhausted spiritually, and only the frequent expressions of true gratitude and love counteract the poison of praise. I realize with such complete conviction my badness and poverty that I shall probably not be deeply wounded by vanity; however, I feel slightly affected, although still in general preserving soberness and balance of soul. As usual, an increase of tension, of attendance at divine services, of interviews and work produces at the same time an increase of spiritual strength.

†

It is always painful for me to 'speak'—I am tormented before and after. It is hard to say the things that are most important, and if I master myself and manage to say some of these 'most important'

---

[1] On the occasion of Father Alexander's appointment to the Russian Cathedral in Paris.

things, it so seldom goes home to others. In general, I am deeply conscious of the pointlessness of all verbal communication. But here, in the youth camp, I speak easily and freely, and do not regret it afterwards.

Especially, I realize how much they need such communication. Though they have quite a sober, practical and elementary approach to life—and, to put it bluntly, a lack of education and culture both interior and exterior—they have an alert intelligence, straightforwardness, a thirst for life, and when someone shows sincere interest and love towards them, they sense it immediately and are grateful.

†

My dislike and distrust of verbal methods of persuasion—and of eloquence in general—is constantly increasing. 'Let your adorning be the hidden man of the heart, in that which is not corruptible, even the ornament of a meek and quiet spirit, which is in the sight of God of great price' (1 Peter iii. 4).

†

Two of Father Alexander's last notes

Time flows by, the greater part of life is gone already, perhaps the best part. What has been accomplished? The summing up: make haste to do good.

†

Think of good and evil, not in terms of outward acts, but of forces operating within us. . . .

†

From Father Alexander's notes and letters
shortly before his death

What a school of humility sickness is! It makes us see that we are poor, naked, and blind.

X comes to see me and rebukes me gently but insistently for my lack of faith and inability to surmount sickness by means of spiritual forces. His argument: Christ has freed us from the slavery of the flesh (Rom. viii). How shall I answer this?

The Christian gift of healing is not something all-powerful, nor a victory over nature.

Many righteous men suffered up to the very end of their lives from diseases which remained uncured—St. Ambrose, Pascal.

The Apostle himself was sick while curing others (not everyone).

How can this be explained? By the fact that so long as we live in this body of death, we bear all its consequences—until the final restoration of all things.

And secondly: 'Always bearing about in the body the dying of the Lord Jesus' (2 Cor. iv. 10).

†

I have thought many things over and re-experienced many things during this illness. Our life is a frightening, insecure and uncertain thing: only the thinnest tissue protects us from pain, suffering, death. And a man is so helpless in face of all this darkness, the whole life of his spirit is so weak: it cannot withstand a temperature of 104°, and breaks down when pain is acute. In general, illness humbles one considerably; the Lord does not leave us without His comfort, but we realize so clearly our own helplessness. We have only one defence against all the horrors surrounding us: a faithful love of Christ, a constant holding fast on to Him.

†

Illness has taught me a great deal. It has confirmed me even more deeply in the conviction that if a man is with Christ, then he is with suffering, and that there is no other way for the Christian than the way of pain, inward and outward. And as I thought of the infinite suffering in the world, I said to myself that through such undeserved, innocent suffering the invisible Kingdom of God is built up, His suffering Body—the Church of Christ—is created and gathered together into unity.

Extracts from Letters to Young People

IF you really wish to place yourself under my direction, I will give you the following advice:

Pray in the morning and in the evening, even if you only recite one single prayer, even if it is only for one or two minutes; but try to achieve complete concentration on the words of the prayer, and to purge your mind from all other preoccupations, attaining a certain warmth of heart—however feeble—a warmth actually felt in the region of the heart, for we pray primarily with our heart.

Read whenever you can, but at any rate each day, one or two verses of the Gospels, and as you do so, make an effort to apply what you read to your life, to your appreciation of the world around you, that is, make an effort to understand what you read as the living word of God, addressed specifically to yourself.

Always read some spiritual work, the biography of a saint, some book on Church history. Here, French books may be useful, books on St. Francis of Assisi or St. Teresa, if you have no Orthodox ones.

Regarding each of these various points, endless developments and further explanations are possible; I have only touched slightly on these subjects. . . .

†

In answer to your questions about fasting: fasting is not hunger. The diabetic, the fakir, the yogi, the prisoner in his cell and the ordinary beggar also feel hunger. Nowhere in the services of Lent do we find fasting mentioned by itself in the usually accepted sense of the word, that is in the sense of not eating meat, etc. Everywhere we find the same appeal: 'Brethren, let us fast bodily and spiritually.' Thus fasting can have a religious meaning only when linked to spiritual exercises. Fasting = exhaustion, refinement. The normal, physiological man, full of well-being, is inaccessible to the influence of higher forces. Fasting disturbs and unsettles this physical well-being of man; he thus becomes more accessible to the influence of the other world, and accepts within himself what is spiritual.

†

. . . About confession—do not put it off. A weak faith and doubts are no obstacle. Go to confession without fail, repenting of weak faith and doubts, admitting them as a sign of your helplessness and sinfulness. Only the blessed, those whose spirit is full of strength, possess complete faith: how can we, impure and unbelieving, hope to possess their faith? If we had it, we would be saintly, strong, godlike, and would not need the help offered us by the Church. And so, you too—do not decline this help.

†

I looked through with disgust several small books of detective stories which are devoured by modern youth. They are dominated by a quite open and obvious idea, which is continuously and persistently inculcated: the stupidity, boredom, and mediocrity of all that belongs to order, to the State, and the attractiveness, beauty, noble character and brilliant talents of those who represent vice and crime. The reader grows consciously accustomed to such combinations as the 'gentleman-burglar', 'the noble murderer', 'the crook, romantically in love'. This is real poison which is, I am sure, intentionally prepared.

†

Read continually such works as feed your soul, and direct you to the one true goal in life. Here, a certain asceticism, self-limitation, self-coercion, are necessary. *Every Christian is an ascetic.* Keep this in mind. Human nature is so distorted that you will have to exercise a ruthless pressure upon it, if you want to straighten it out according to the Gospel measures, and you will have to do this straightening out every day, every hour. May God help you in this task. . . .

†

The chief mistake of our young people is their conviction that everything can be understood, that Christianity is a philosophical system which can be logically proved and expressed, and that in their present state (moral, religious, intellectual) they are capable of grasping every truth of the faith. They often stubbornly refuse to see that Christianity is a *life*. Instead of loving the truth and bowing down before it, they discuss, enter into polemics.

†

I am convinced that in our condition of life the *daily* reading of the Holy Fathers and of the Lives of the Saints is the essential and most effective means of sustaining our faith and love. This reading helps us to form a concrete picture of the realm to which we aspire, it provides our faith with images, ideas, feelings, shows us the way, gives us hope by describing the various steps and stages of the interior life, warms the heart and draws us towards the blessed life of the saints. How can we love that which we do not see, of which we receive no constant impression? The early Christians were filled with such great faith and love because they had heard, and seen with their eyes, and their hands had handled (1 John i. 1). This possibility of receiving direct impressions from the Divine Light is granted to us either through communion with living saints or through that very same communion, obtained from reading and penetrating into their inner life. It might seem that we can attain this same aim by reading the Gospels. Indeed we can—provided we are capable of reading them with profit. But there are many people to whom the Gospels mean nothing—either because they were 'bored' by the Gospels in childhood or because the light of the Gospels is too bright for weak eyes, and not everyone is able to apprehend it. In this case, one needs the gentler atmosphere of the Lives of the Saints, which are penetrated with the same evangelical light, but in a more accessible form.

†

You ask the meaning of the text: 'Except a corn of wheat fall into the ground and die . . .' etc. (John xii. 24).

What is here understood is the death of our baser personality, of our selfishness, 'self', wilfulness—only when these are destroyed, is there born within us a new and blessed life, which illumines everyone and 'bringeth forth much fruit'. This is what Goethe says: 'Entbehren sollst du, sollst entbehren.'[1] And this is what St. Seraphim meant when he said: 'My joy, acquire a peaceful spirit, and thousands of people will find salvation near you.' That is, acquire peace and quiet in your soul, the absence of anger, of passion—and you will illumine the path of all who come near you.

†

---

[1] Thou shalt deprive thyself.

What I said and wrote to you about obedience must not be understood as a sort of spinelessness, as an unloading of one's own responsibility onto the shoulders of others, a giving-up of one's own path.

No—obedience is an ascetic feat, an ascetic feat of the utmost difficulty, demanding perhaps a greater force of character (however paradoxical this may sound) than living according to one's own wishes.

†

I advise you to keep a diary. This helps one to study oneself, saves one from making the same mistakes, keeps the past alive. It is worth while noting every great joy, sorrow, every important encounter, every book which has impressed us, our tastes, hopes, desires.

†

Permit me to offer you some advice:

The most radical remedy against pride is to live in obedience—to parents, friends, your spiritual adviser.

Make yourself listen attentively to the advice and the opinion of others. Do not be in a hurry to believe in the truth of the ideas that come to our mind.

Be more simple with other people, do not suspect their words and ideas of containing some special, hidden meaning.

Do not evade games, gaiety, society.

Pray as often as possible: 'Lord, grant me patience, generosity and meekness'; or '. . . humility, chastity and obedience.'

May God help you to acquire the fruits of the Holy Ghost, the first of which are love, joy, peace, longsuffering (Gal. v. 22).

†

Be patient in your sorrows: even the lower creatures cannot live without suffering; and the nobler man is the more he suffers.

†

The motives which lead people to start smoking are mean and vulgar—wanting to be like the others, fear of being laughed at, the desire to gain greater prestige: the psychology of a coward and a crook combined. This leads to estrangement from family and friends. Aesthetically speaking, this vulgarity is especially insufferable in girls. Psychologically speaking, smoking opens the door to all that is forbidden and sinful.

Smoking, and every other form of narcosis, obscures our sense of purity and chastity. Our first cigarette is already our first fall, the loss of our purity. It is not false puritanism but an immediate feeling and a deep conviction, which lead me to say this to you. Ask any smoker—the beginning of smoking was for him, in a sense, a fall.

†

Be simpler and gayer. The Christian must certainly not cut a gloomy figure, and appear exhausted by ascetic practices, a living reproach to others. Even if you are sincere, you will not be able to keep it up, and you will be in danger of going by way of reaction to the opposite extreme. Do not bother about appearances—they should be the natural result of inner life, and manifest themselves spontaneously.

†

. . . You are embarrassed by your shyness and timidity in your relations with people. Little by little, practice will develop a certain insolent self-confidence, if this is any consolation to you.

But, essentially, this self-confidence is a striking proof of the vanity which exists in us.

†

What must we do in order not to be bored with people? We must understand that God accomplishes His will concerning us through the persons whom He sends us. There are no accidental meetings: either God sends us a person we need or we are sent to someone by God, without our being aware of it.

We implore God's help, and when He manifests it through some particular person we reject it out of carelessness, inattention, rudeness.

†

You ask me about the 'strait gate' and 'narrow way' (Matt. vii. 14): why must they be strait and narrow? Why cannot there be an easy life here also, in the Church?

They have to be strait and narrow because of the corruption, the maiming of human nature by sin and death. Sufferings have both a positive power and a meaning. Man grows spiritually, if he meets them readily and courageously. It is impossible to live easily and happily in this present world of sufferings.

†

I think that two causes are at the basis of your spiritual difficulties: 1. An excessive preoccupation with your own self, and, as a result, an insufficient interest in those around you. 2. An insufficient love of Christ. This love is the basis and root of all spiritual life and strength; we must make it grow up and must train it in ourselves. Begin, for instance, with the overwhelming thought that in all human history there has never been anything more beautiful than Christ. Take all the Napoleons, Caesars, Alexanders, all the geniuses and leaders of humanity—and you will find in all of them blemishes and impurity; only in Mary's meek son you will behold all that is beautiful, all that is desirable, all that humanity has ever dreamt of. To gaze attentively at this image, to understand its meaning and to root it deeply in ourselves, to feed on the thought of Him, to give our heart to Him—such is the life of the Christian. When this happens, then there is complete peace of heart, that peace of which St. Isaac the Syrian said: 'Be at peace with yourself, and heaven and earth will be at peace with you.'

†

You ask me, what is essential in religion if it is not the moral element? The sacraments, the dogmas and ritual, and—more especially—real union with God and the preparation of our soul for immortality; all these are no less important.

†

Regarding the religious views of Tolstoy and Rousseau, we may put things as follows. Religion is a complex affair. Wine, for instance, is composed of water, alcohol, aromatic and colouring essences, etc. The same is true of religion. It contains the alcohol of dogma, the aromatic essences of worship and ritual, while the moral rules are water. Tolstoy and Rousseau saw only water.

†

The problem of choosing a career is very difficult, but if you are conscious of a clearly expressed vocation, this voice should be obeyed above all. Even from the practical point of view, it is better to choose what you feel specially called to do. The choice of a career not prompted by a vocation but due to secondary reasons, always produces second class workers, neither talented nor inspired.

†

You have good reason to feel sorry that you cannot apprehend God: for one of God's attributes is precisely to be inconceivable. Indeed, if it were possible for us finite creatures to comprehend God, this would mean that God is limited and finite–in other words, that the deity is incomplete. Generally speaking our powers of knowledge are insufficient for the task of knowing the Divine, and we must not be too quick to mistake our limitations for limitations in what we desire to know. We bear an immortal, divine soul, which despite all its limitations tends naturally towards God. Our error is to make judgements about God, while being ourselves outside God. In human affairs we would never put up with such presumption. No one would undertake to cure without having studied medicine, or to build houses without acquiring special knowledge. How is it then that men, who stand far away from the divine realm, yet judge it with great severity? And at the same time, how humble are those who have made progress in the knowledge of God! One might say that men's boldness in making judgements about God varies in inverse proportion to their closeness to Him.

†

You are unsuccessful in your reading of the Gospels, because, in the first place, you lack sufficient imagination. The words of the Gospels do not give you a vivid image of Christ; in order to obtain it, you need to make a real effort of your own. Secondly, you do not love Christ enough, or else with the greatest eagerness you would read over and over again this, the one and only book that testifies to Him, and you would never stop discovering new details and shades of meaning in it.

There are two ways of reading the Gospels:

1. To read very little at a time—a verse or two—then to read them over again, reflecting on them all day long, considering them as words of Christ addressed *to you* personally.

2. When you know the Gospels well, to read large portions of them (one Evangelist at a time, or all four together), in order to grasp the sequence of events and the general spirit. If you have a weak memory, this is a great help: indeed, it is even essential.

†

I understand quite well your complaints about the emptiness of the life around you. I shall recommend two things to you: first, short prayer, frequently repeated, in the middle of the day, recited to yourself whilst walking: something like 'Lord, purify me, a sinner . . .' 'Lord Christ, Son of God, forgive me . . .' repeated many times. This is a means of preserving the memory of God, which will defend you against frivolousness, chatter, etc.

And secondly: not to hide your religious convictions too much from your friends. You may unexpectedly meet people who sympathize, who are interested and eager to question you. In a word, do not try to hide your true nature from others under the common mask of frivolity and emptiness.

†

Our task, the task of Orthodox Russian people, is to understand our faith in two ways: by becoming familiar with it, and by living by it. You put a series of questions to me, but remember that theological and philosophical questions cannot be examined in an arbitrary order and sequence, just as in mathematics and other sciences.

If you want to understand our faith thoroughly, you must read the Gospels with commentaries in hand, and live according to the rules of the Church. Until you do this, you will just be indulging in intellectual games and idle curiosity. I know how impracticable my suggestions are, and how easy and diverting it is, on the other hand, to read the fantasies of theosophy, but I can advise you nothing else.

†

You ask me about the outward forms in religion. But what more is there to be said about it beyond what Christ said: 'And why call ye me, Lord, Lord, and do not the things which I say?' (Luke vi. 46). I think that all over-emphasis on the aesthetic element in religious worship is an infraction of the third commandment. Aesthetic emotion bears such a close resemblance to religious emotion, that it is easy to make a mistake. And in general, wherever there is a 'passionate' attitude, there is something dubious. One must be careful not to infringe inner truthfulness.

†

When you feel that you have the right to condemn some occurrence or action that is utterly revolting, test yourself: do you not at the same time feel personal anger, irritation, jealousy, hostility toward men, the desire to mock, to humiliate? You will nearly always find that these feelings exist. The conclusion to be drawn is clear.

†

You speak of 'religious minimalism'. But in the Gospels, you will find no other point of view except the combination *maximalism* in spiritual things with *minimalism* in the things of ordinary life

('Be ye therefore perfect as your Father which is in heaven', 'Take no thought for your life, what ye shall eat, or what ye shall drink', etc.). Whatever the subtle arguments we offer in order to interpret these words, clearly and directly addressed to us, we can extract no other meaning from them. The only way to make these words not binding on us is to make the Gospels themselves not binding— and that is to deny Christ. But do these words mean that we must immediately give up our work, our comfortable homes, our children, our family, our small everyday joys, and issue forth, like homeless tramps, wherever our footsteps lead us? That would be a wrong solution of the problem—wrong, because external. We must begin by seeking such a state within our own soul that external decisions will come spontaneously—a state in which constant 'joy in our Lord' and the power of grace imperiously dictate to us another mode of life, instead of the selfish, epicurean existence which we lead at present. Until then, it is enough to feel sorrow and pain because of our spiritual poverty and wretchedness, because of our pettiness, degradation, lack of faith, spiritual laziness —and not to make of these vices our principle and rule of life. If I suspected that you have drawn up for yourself a programme of petty, humdrum occupations, with a maximum of pleasures and a minimum of spiritual life, I would feel very anxious. But this, of course, is not the case: surely, you feel an inner anxiety about yourself, grief for Russia and the Church, desire for that which is exalted, righteous and saintly, and readiness to sacrifice yourself, and you also feel your spiritual weakness. Thank God for that!

†

What shall we do to avoid feeling angry and offended, when we are insulted and injured? Must we bear it, clenching our teeth? Must we train our self-control and develop our patience? This is all right in itself, but yet it is not the real thing: it is only an exterior, non-Christian way, devoid of grace. The only true way is to keep in mind constantly and every minute the exalted goal we are pursuing, to 'set the Lord always before me: because He is at my right hand' (Psalm xvi. 8), as the psalmist puts it. . . .

Do you remember this story about Clemenceau? One day, as he was inspecting the trenches, he came up to a soldier from behind and, tapping him on the shoulder, asked: 'Well, old man, how are you getting on?' The soldier, without turning his head and not knowing who was addressing him, kicked him and swore foully. Clemenceau, who never forgave an offence, only smiled and went on his way. Where did this pagan, this passionate and hot-tempered man, find the necessary patience and meekness in bearing offences? In the great idea which he kept continually before him: the victory of France. So let us too be preserved from sin by the constant thought of the victory of Him who has overcome the world. When we are depressed by an offence, when we are angry, our sin consists in the fact that at that moment our heart has lost its faith and love of Christ, and that we have fallen short of the lofty goal which our calling as Christians requires of us; at that moment, we have grown so narrow in our outlook that we can only remember the letter which we were writing before we were disturbed, the book which we wanted to read, a thousand trifles which have wounded us, and above all we think of ourselves—all the time of ourselves. 'I have set the Lord always before me: because he is at my right hand' (Psalm xvi. 8). This is the only path, so may God confirm you in it.

†

You try to justify yourself, saying that the fault you have committed is small and of no importance. But in the world there is nothing small and of no importance, whether good or bad. The most insignificant action, a word spoken at random, the most fleeting feeling—all these are important and real, just as everything is real in the world. And so everything, however small, must correspond to the chief thing in our life, and nothing must be considered beneath our attention or outside the scope of our responsibility.

†

Common (youthful) errors in the practice of theology:
1. The assumption that all questions can be solved.
2. The conviction that the solution of these questions is a purely intellectual, discursive process: that is, a process independent of inner, spiritual effort, of the purifying of the heart and the mind, of prayer.

†

Many youthful doubts stem from pride:
1. 'I must do something decisive, so as to make an end to all compromise and give God everything.'
2. 'I must not receive frequent communion—I am unworthy.'
3. The proud feeling of one's extraordinary sinfulness.
4. 'I should not get married, I would be taking too much upon myself in creating new beings.'

†

The words in the Gospel about the family should not be understood literally. We know that the apostles—Peter, for example—lived with their families, that Lazarus and his sisters did not forsake each other, but received Christ in their family, while still remaining true to Him. We know many saints who were family men. What is required is simply to put family relations in the second place in one's soul, to be ready at any moment to put one's faith in the first place. It is the same as with property: 'As having nothing, and yet possessing all things' (2 Cor. vi. 10).

†

. . . You write of the 'cold and solitude' of your life. I long to comfort you! But is it possible that prayers, friends, work, do not release you from solitude and do not warm your heart? I am convinced that this does happen to you on occasion, and that your words mean that *sometimes*, and even *often*, you feel cold and solitary; often, but not always. Of course, the circumstances of your life play an important part in this solitude, but let us be brave and confess that a certain part of this solitude, and even perhaps the greater part, is due to yourself. You admit that it is difficult for you to 'come out of yourself'. I mean that there is in you a certain concentration on yourself; and this is a sin—not just a small one, but a fundamental and primary sin in our human nature. 'We have fallen into *self-lust*, preferring contemplation of self to the contemplation of God' (St. Athanasius the Great).[1] The escape from this state, from this concentration on self, can be found by opening up oneself and going out to meet the Objective. Seek for blessed simplicity and pray for it, for that holy simplicity which is obtained through self-forgetfulness, through turning completely, unreservedly, to the divine Light, to the world, to our brethren. Then full peace and joy and rest will descend upon your soul. The path to these things is obedience—swift, voluntary, joyful, unreasoning. You may ask: obedience to whom? To the first person you come across, to your relations, to the voice of conscience, to the rules of the Church, to your spiritual director. To be wrapped in ourselves is always a sin, but not always our own *personal* sin; in many cases it is the vice of our entire race, family, ancestors. But when this is so, we have even greater reason to struggle against this sin, in order to save our entire race: for every personal acquisition in the spiritual realm is mysteriously communicated to all our relations, alive or dead. Our Lord will clearly show this through your own experience, if you advance along this path. It has been granted to you to understand these questions better than to all the other

---

[1] Athanasius, bishop of Alexandria (295–373), opponent of Arianism and one of the greatest of the Greek Fathers.

members of your family, and if through prayer you obtain from God meekness, peace of the soul and patience, you will draw all your family into the same spiritual path, and you will achieve this not by preaching and teaching but by silent improvement in what is good. . . .

†

Allow me to say something about your reading. All that you have read until now was for the development and the strengthening of your Christian thought, your Christian outlook. But this is not enough; not only is it not enough, but such kind of reading should decidedly become secondary. Christianity is not a philosophical system, it is *life*, a special way of life, and this must be studied continuously—literally every day. There are masters of this divine life who started with the first steps and who attained such lofty heights that one does not always understand them when they speak about these summits. You must read them. They are, of course, the Holy Fathers, the ascetics, heroes, giants in their faith and zeal for life in God. Here are the chief figures, roughly in historical order: Saint Antony the Great, Ephrem the Syrian, Abba Dorotheus, Macarius the Great,[1] Saint John of the Ladder, Isaac the Syrian, Simeon the New Theologian. First one may read our Russian authors—Innocent, Ignatius Bryanchaninov, Theophan the Recluse,[2] John of Kronstadt. They are steeped in the spirit of the Fathers I mentioned just now, but express it in the language of our time, applying it to the conditions of our life. Many of the ascetic fathers are collected in the various volumes of the

---

[1] Antony of Egypt (251–356), hermit and father of Christian monasticism; Ephrem the Syrian (died 373), the greatest writer of the Syrian Church; Dorotheus (sixth century), abbot of a monastery near Gaza in Palestine; Macarius the Great (died *ca.* 390), monk of Scetis in Egypt.

[2] Russian spiritual writers of the nineteenth century.

Philokalia,[1] in roughly the right sequence. One should read them slowly, taking notes and meditating on them, taking two or three months over one volume.

†

In our understanding of the word of God one may distinguish the following stages: hearing, understanding, the acceptance in our heart of what we hear and, finally, its application to our life. Examine yourself—at which of these stages are you at present? Do you always go even so far as to listen to God's word? Do you often read it? Hearing or reading it, do you take the trouble to penetrate its meaning, in order to understand it? Does it reach your conscience, your heart? Does it stir them? If so, has it yielded fruit, does it move you to action, breaking up the apathy of our normal, self-contented life? Examine yourself—and slowly, persistently, begin to ascend these steps.

†

I have read with compassion and sympathy the list of your spiritual tribulations, and have suffered with you. And yet, I believe in the fundamental goodness of your soul. The fact is, it is very difficult to live according to conscience, and it is very easy to live in the same way as everybody else, just taking things as they come. There is an excellent Russian proverb: 'What belongs to God is expensive; what belongs to the devil is cheap.' And everyone rushes to buy these cheap goods. How easy it is to live without effort, in the constant cinema show of encounters and conversations, without taking any obligations on oneself, without forcing

---

[1] The *Philokalia* is a large collection of spiritual writings, dating from the fourth to the fifteenth century, compiled by a Greek monk, St. Nicodemus of the Holy Mountain (1748–1809), and first published in 1782. A Russian translation in five volumes, under the title *Dobrotolyubie*, appeared in 1876–90. Large parts of it have appeared in English translation.

oneself to do anything, but just feeding one's conceit, laziness, and frivolity. But I am firmly convinced that deep down in your heart you feel a repulsion for such a life, that you would like to be kind and attentive to everyone, luminous, pure.

Let me give you a little advice. Begin each day in the following way (of course if the necessary conditions exist): first of all, before starting any of the day's work, spend at least half an hour in prayer, reading and reflection. When praying, remember all those who are dear to you, the sick, the dead, and turn to God for help in your inner and exterior difficulties. Then read. It would be well if, besides the Gospels, you read some passages from a spiritual work. Then reflect upon the coming day, represent to yourself all the possible difficulties which are awaiting you, prepare yourself to meet them, and, above all, promise yourself every morning not to commit a single action against your conscience. And in the evening, even when already lying in bed, pass in review the day you have just spent, examining it from the standpoint of this rule. I know how difficult it is, but try; this is the real, direct path to a full spiritual amendment. And write and tell me whether anything has come out of it.

†

. . . Be wise, and extract from the trials which God has sent you a maximum of advantages for yourself. What is the good of having read whole libraries full of the works of wise men, philosophers, theologians, and still in real life to stumble at every step—'these shall receive greater damnation' (Mark xii. 40). In *Vekhi*, Gershenzon[1] wrote: 'We all know so many divine truths that one

---

[1] *Vekhi* ('Signposts'), a religious symposium published in 1909 by members of the Russian intelligentsia: the work created a great stir at the time, representing as it did an abandonment, by leading writers, of the anti-religious bias which had hitherto characterized the Russian intelligentsia.

Mikhail Gershenzon (1869–1925) was one of the seven contributors: among the others were Berdyaev and Bulgakov.

thousandth part of what we know would suffice to make saints of us; but to be aware of truth and to live according to truth are, as we all know, two very different things.' And so, do not let yourself follow only the easy path – the path of collecting and developing knowledge – but plunge the metal of your plough more deeply in your heart. The conditions with which God has surrounded us are the only possible way of salvation for us; these conditions will change as soon as we have made full use of them, having transformed the bitterness of offences, illnesses, labours, into the gold of patience, absence of anger, meekness. Do not let your soul be divided in such a way that one part of it soars to the seventh heaven with Dionysius the Areopagite,[1] while the other part crawls on the ground in depression, petty susceptibility – and perhaps in anger.

†

You must keep yourself pure and bright, so that your light shines for others. And in order to achieve this, you must love the light and not betray it: 'Now are ye light in the Lord: walk as children of light' (Eph. v. 8). And in practice, what must we do? Seek this light in yourself and others, sustain and cultivate in yourself and others the smallest spark of good and light, rejoice in the light, do not even believe in darkness and falsehood, close your eyes on them, for they are spectres which swell up from the attention we give to them. . . .

†

What is the use of faith? No use at all. If I said that it is useful insofar as it serves to make man good, to teach him to help others, to know God and save his soul – all this would imply an interested, selfish attitude towards faith. We do not believe in order to gain

---

[1] St. Paul's convert at Athens (Acts xvii. 34), traditionally regarded as the author of various mystical writings.

this or that, we believe because we love God, because God – in His manifestation on earth as the Incarnate Christ – constitutes all that is most luminous, pure, infinitely beautiful – in a word, the sum total of all that is most desirable. Love of God leads to faith in God. When you seek for truth among contradictory philosophic systems, you do so because you love the Truth; if earthly beauty lies heavy on your heart and does not satisfy you, it is because we can find peace only in the Eternal and Incorruptible Beauty. If the impurity of your heart tortures you, it is because, without being aware of it, you thirst for absolute purity and saintliness.

†

You complain that your life is 'rough and rugged'. But whatever we do is always like that. Where there are men, there are passions, narrowmindedness, selfishness, conceit. Thus it is all the more necessary for us to maintain ourselves at a certain depth, to keep in mind the all-embracing, final goal before us, to destroy in ourselves all that is petty and trivial: then we shall find it easier to suffer all these faults in others. O God, send us patience, generosity, meekness. We are all working, not for ourselves, but for God: and therefore all conflicts will be settled, not through our own great efforts, but through God's wisdom.

†

The fact that you feel the weight of your life proves that there is in your soul a shining light which is horrified at all this constant falsehood, impurity, and pettiness. Each of us is a twofold being: on the one hand, deserving judgement and condemnation; on the other, judging and thirsting for truth and light. The more the inner man grows in you, the more light you will behold in all the things and people that surround you, until you attain such purity of heart that everything around you will appear luminous and transfigured: this is to live in paradise even before death. It is the condition of the righteous and saints; there are many of them among us, but we do not see them, because of the impurity of our eyes and hearts. I mean, we see them, but they appear to us either quite ordinary people, or else eccentrics and cranks.

†

The danger of self-willed ascetic exercises: because of our extreme physical and sensual density and weight, we are not easily penetrated by the action of the spiritual world. The 'sounds of heaven'[1] will reach us only if our body has been refined. But the devil is also a spirit. The sensual, heavy man is equally impenetrable to the influence of both worlds. By refining his body through self-willed ascetic exercises, a man renders it accessible to the evil spirits as well as to God.

†

. . . I shall not answer your request in full, but shall only write what I have often said and written to my spiritual children.

I am unable – and, indeed, consider it wrong – to take it on myself to decide someone else's destiny or family affairs. I do not feel called to the role of a *starets* and I recognize my profound unworthiness to be such. In general, *starchestvo*[2] and 'obedience' imply too great a responsibility and are far too difficult for both parties, to be undertaken on a sudden impulse.

†

---

[1] A phrase used by the Russian writer Mikhail Lermontov (1814–41) in one of his poems.

[1] *Starchestvo*: the ministry of spiritual direction exercised by a *starets* (see above, p. 29, n. 1.

Talking about a feeling kills that very feeling.

†

If the heart is cold and prayer is difficult, we must turn to the Gospels; if this does not help, turn to your favourite Holy Father; each of us should possess a special 'friend' among the saints.

†

You complain that reading the Holy Fathers is difficult and even bores you. But try to tell yourself that it is not *they* who are difficult and boring, but it is your soul which perhaps is not properly prepared to see the light which others behold. Do not, however, give up this reading, but try to warm your heart with the warmth of their faith, try to enter into contact with their spiritual experience. You may object that there is too great a discrepancy between the heights on which they move and the pettiness of everyday life which holds us imprisoned. But watch closely—it cannot be that you *always* experience *only* difficulty and boredom. At rare moments of life—in ordeal and sorrow, or in great joy—the soul seeks to rise; and then, perhaps, the words which hitherto failed to touch you will acquire a different sound. At ordinary times, on the other hand, hard work is necessary and a certain violence must be exercised on oneself, in order to arouse oneself from sloth. Rest assured—these efforts will yield their fruit, and the accumulation of spiritual riches, which for the present remain invisible to you, will manifest itself when the right time comes and perhaps will save you when in real trouble.

You also write of your solitude and loneliness. Of course, you need a living contact with other people and the feeling of their nearness. But think: what 'select company' you enjoy in these Holy Fathers, what treasures of the highest souls, accumulated over centuries, are granted you in full possession. Herein lies the joy of fellowship in the Church—we are all alive, all brothers in the Church, and so a living member of the Church cannot feel lonely and cut off.

†

Individual effort is fruitless in so many cases. Seek friendship. This is a case when 1 + 1 are not 2, but at least 3 : the two of you, plus that great power—mutual love—which will sustain and fortify you.

†

Usually we live on the most superficial levels of our soul and consciousness. This is obvious, for instance, in the fact that we are so easily moved to indignation by petty reasons, and attach such a great importance to worthless objects. Half of our sorrows and difficulties would disappear, if we shifted the centre of our interests to a greater depth. If I recommend to you with such insistence the reading of the Gospels, especially in the morning, it is because this exercise will give a different tone to the beginning of each day, and will help you to spend it in a more worthy way. It will help you to keep your heart at peace, whatever the storms of life which await you in the coming day.

†

Every task, even the smallest, you must begin with a prayer, appealing to God's power for help in this duty which faces you: you must make an act of raising it to a higher level. Then you will not, and cannot, commit any bad action.

†

Our discussions and public lectures, with lecturers chosen at random and casual audiences, are not living organisms but a mechanical, artificial product; nobody has put his heart in it or suffered in labour to create it, nobody loves it as a parent. But small groups with a constant attendance, with a leader who knows all the listeners, are quite different: this is something organic that provides guidance and education. This, of course, applies especially to youth groups.

†

Here are a few impressions from my contact with youth. The young people who grew up under the impact of revolution, war, and emigration, are often nervously unstable, but practical and realistic; they have but little experience of what is good; they are often not particularly cultured, but display a peculiar honesty and straightforwardness, rejecting pretentious words and 'ideals' without deeds. They are sensitive to falsehood.

Are they being kept in reserve for Russia, and how are we to preserve them? But youth has the right to ask: what for? They do not want to devote their lives to some goal invented by old people.

They want to live for themselves. People can and do live as someone else's pale shadow, a copy, a third-class product. But this, of course, is a poor expedient. The first and primary meaning of existence is to be oneself.

But a person is a complex structure, and nationality plays an important part, if not openly then subconsciously, and this at times shows up in ways that take us quite by surprise.

And so, if we want to be ourselves, we must be Russians.

But can one not be completely transformed into an Englishman, a German, a Frenchman? Only in part.

Otherwise, it is a long masquerade, draining our strength, not giving us the power to create.

But where shall we seek that which is truly Russian? What has preserved great nations? What protected or destroyed them? Language and faith. And faith more than language.

. . . And so I would like to say to our youth: you are young, you have the wings of youth, you will be able to accomplish this heroic deed—to remain Orthodox and Russian. You are Orthodox, all the treasures of the Church are at your service—her prayers, her sacraments: learn to know these treasures, study them, be nourished by them.

You are Russians. All that your forefathers accumulated, all the cultural heritage, the entire genius of a very great nation—this is your property which has been given to you free. Your duty is to study this heritage, to cultivate it in yourselves, to participate in the common Russian cause.

But it is hard indeed to achieve anything by individual efforts: often they are quite sterile. Strength lies in *sobornost*,[1] in friendship. Youth organizations, helping young people to keep together, are thus of the greatest importance.

†

And one last remark—nearly all young men are moody, gloomy, and clumsy. In all girls, there is light-heartedness, simplicity, and a kind of radiance. For them, everything seems easier; when they turn to Christianity, they attain more easily the warmheartedness springing from such a conversion. Young men have much more to overcome: first of all—reasoning, self-love, and so on. This is why an important role will probably be reserved for women in the future revival of the Russian Church.

---

[1] See above, p. 87, n. 1.

Advice to Young Priests

PASTORAL work must be individual and creative.

†

A method often practised becomes routine.

†

Every sermon, every lesson, has meaning and value only when it is the result of personal spiritual experience and knowledge. Every sermon pronounced only with our lips is dead and false, and those who listen always unmistakably feel it.

†

'Pastoral texts' (I copy them out for guidance):
'We were gentle among you, even as a nurse cherisheth her children' (1 Thess. ii. 7).
'I am made all things to all men, that I might by all means save some' (1 Cor. ix. 22).

†

We must teach people how to make their confession. How often, instead of a confession, one hears only worldly chatter, boasting, the quoting of flattering opinions about the penitent's character, complaints about the family and about the difficulties of life. This is partly the result of ignorance, of an absence of religious culture; and it is partly the result of sinful entanglement and weakness, when a man does not know how to see himself and does not even try to do so, when he has neither the habit nor the desire to analyse his soul, when he feels no revulsion against sin, no attraction towards the light, no thirst for purification.

†

Try to bring it about that all who come to confession take away with them at least one good habit—for instance, an obligatory prayer twice a day, a prayer at noon, abstaining from judging others, etc. This good habit must be insistently grafted, we must constantly check up on it, and then it becomes a necessity.

†

The penitent preparing for confession sometimes experiences a fear of sin, sincere remorse and tears; yet, when he stands before the priest, he feels nothing, no fear, no contrition. Would it not be possible to enlarge the scope of the sacraments? Can one not consider that the sacrament of penitence includes all remorse, all prayers and feelings of contrition, so that the actual confession is but a conclusion—even though it is the most important moment?

†

Every priest must be well informed about nervous and psychic diseases—this is absolutely necessary in pastoral practice.

A common case: the penitent who comes to confession and the priest who acts as confessor both mistake a purely nervous phenomenon for a religious experience; or else the priest fails to recognize the hysterical undercurrent beneath certain expressions, and thus only makes the situation worse. And often the opposite also happens: a painful condition of the soul, weighed down by sin, entangled and confused by unresolved conflicts, is mistaken for nervous disease. We know of cases when one single confession was sufficient to wipe out supposedly deep-rooted nervous diseases which no medical treatment could cure.

A person who goes to confession often, and who does not accumulate a great weight of sin on his soul, cannot be otherwise than healthy. Confession is a salutary unburdening of the soul. In this respect confession is of immense significance, as also is a life supported by the saving succour of the Church.

†

Does not a first confession, if made prematurely—some children of six are practically infants—interfere with the child's simplicity, wholesomeness, spontaneity, by intruding an artificially created self-analysis? For some, particularly 'childish' children, I would put off confession for a year or two.

†

Today, some children of 10–12 years old asked me (evidently after a great discussion among themselves): what is asceticism? I answered: a system of exercises which submits the body to the spirit. 'And what are the first exercises of all?'

1. Breathe through the nose. 2. Eat without filling yourself (don't take a second helping). 3. Don't lie about in bed.

This could be the special theme of a long talk with children.

†

We allow frequent confession and communion, yet we sometimes forget the saving force of prolonged penitence, which is only possible during Lent, with its many special services. Then, during the course of a week, man goes through a vivid and convincing experience of the struggle against sin and the joy of victory when it is defeated, and sees the result of his prayer.

†

The complicated condition of many penitents, the apparent hopelessness of their situation—'no matter what I do, I shall drop back into the same old faults, I am powerless to struggle against sin'—result from the fact that these people stand *outside* the Church. Their salvation lies in *entering* the Church, in experiencing the communion of love with their brethren. In our Church practice we have forgotten the communal character of our sacraments, and, amongst others, of the sacrament of penitence.

†

I often notice, in those who come to confession, a desire to pass painlessly through the operation: either they are content with generalities, or they speak about trifles, keeping silent about the things which ought really to weigh on their conscience. In such cases we have a false shame in facing the priest and, in general, an irresoluteness, such as one feels before every important action, and especially a cowardly fear at the idea of having seriously to over-turn one's life, full of petty and habitual weaknesses. Real confession, being a beneficial upheaval of the soul, frightens one by its decisive character, by the necessity of changing something, or of simply starting to reflect upon onself. Here the priest must display firmness; he must not be afraid of disturbing this tranquillity, and trying to awaken a feeling of genuine repentance.

†

Over-scrupulous people, suspicious of every movement in their soul, who torture themselves and their spiritual director by a continual petty inquiry into their sins, eventually reach a state of complete confusion. They should be forbidden to analyse themselves and to test their conscience continuously; they must be given a simple, nourishing diet: prayer and good deeds; for it is through these things that simplicity of soul is acquired and the feeling for the Truth is developed. Once this is achieved, self-examination can be resumed.

†

For the unrepentant and hardhearted, I think a public confession in front of the entire congregation would be necessary, as used to be done in the early Church.

†

In our pastoral practice, little attention has been given to how a priest should direct unbalanced, hysterical people, whose psychological state is abnormal. According to my observations, the tension of prayer and the effort of fasting often only contribute to increase their inner chaos; these exercises not only fail to straighten them out, but do them obvious harm. Here personal methods are required, methods sometimes the opposite of those applied to normal people.

†

People often do not know how to approach confession. One must help them, awaken a feeling of repentance in them, put a few leading questions: have they experienced during the recent period any kind of spiritual life (struggle against sin, prayer, self-control, an effort to improve), have they progressed in anything, or fallen back? Which sin do they consider the most important, and which virtue?

†

It is necessary to recommend the reception of the holy sacraments as frequently as possible. A lesson attended only once a year teaches nothing.

†

During confession, what many people—if not all—need most is that the priest should pray with them. This joint prayer softens the heart, sharpens repentance, refines the spiritual sight.

†

Lessons of the past Lent:
However tired you are, show as much attention as possible, do not hurry. It is best to show everyone complete love, forbearance, sympathy, not to frighten anyone away by one's severity.

Even if the penitent's confession is on the wrong lines—if they boast, enumerating their virtues, relating in detail all the circumstances of their life—do not be abrupt, do not interrupt; there are many unfortunate people who come expressly to cry over the hardships of their life.

Read distinctly to the penitent the prayer before confession: 'Touch his heart, open the eyes of his heart, make him, O Lord, to see his faults, grant him sorrow for his sins, the spirit of heartfelt contrition and mortification, that he may be purified and sanctified. . . .' Often after this prayer the indifferent experience a feeling of repentance.

It is essential to secure sincere repentance, if possible tears—for this purpose it is not necessary for the penitent to enter into all the details, yet in order that tears may appear, there is often need for a detailed and concrete account.

†

Prescribe a penance *to everyone*. Penance is a spiritual reminder, a lesson, an exercise; it accustoms us to spiritual effort, awakening a taste for it in us. This penance must be limited by assigning a certain fixed task, for instance, to recite forty *Akathists*[1] or the like (I recall the case of N, who was unwilling to give up the daily recitation of the Akathist, when the time of the penance came to an end). Possible forms of penance—prostrations,[2] recitation of the Jesus Prayer,[3] rising for prayer at midnight, reading, fasting, alms-giving—whatever each requires.

†

Normal order in confession

Prayer, and a short advice about how to make the confession.
Then let the penitent relate his sins in full, without interrupting him; only help him if he is silent.

---

[1] On *akathists*, see above, p. 79, n. 1.

[2] In the Orthodox Church, it is a common practice—particularly in periods of fasting—to prostrate oneself during Church services or private prayers, touching the ground with the forehead and then rising immediately. This may be repeated a number of times, accompanied by the sign of the Cross or short prayers.

[3] The text of the Jesus Prayer runs: 'Lord Jesus Christ, Son of God, have mercy upon me, a sinner' (sometimes the last two words are omitted). It is repeated—often with the help of a rosary—for limited periods or continuously. Its recitation is particularly recommended to monks, but it is also used by many lay people.

Prayer, asking the Lord to send the spirit of heartfelt contrition to the penitent, and to grant him the forgiveness of his sins.
Advice.
Absolution.

†

You cannot cure the soul of others or 'help people', without having changed yourself. You cannot put in order the spiritual economy of others, so long as there is chaos in your own soul. You cannot bring peace to others if you do not have it yourself.

Often, we help other people, not by a series of conscious acts, directed upon their soul, but rather by influencing them through our spiritual gifts, without ourselves seeing or knowing how we do so. Once Antony the Great asked a visitor, who said nothing at all, 'Why do you not ask me anything?' and the other answered, 'It is enough for me to look at you, holy father'.

†

How important clothes are. A whole complex of feelings, ideas, movements of the soul, is linked to clothes, to uniform. In particular, I feel that the priest must not wear civilian clothes. When he removes his priestly garb, he inevitably acquires an 'unpriestly' feeling, and in some measure betrays his priesthood.

†

Every man who is a Christian, and especially the priest, must always be ready to renounce everything in God's name, if God demands it.

†

One must not hesitate to visit even those families which are the most dubious from the viewpoint of the Church. I know from experience that they will be pleased; everywhere you will be received with great joy, they do not let you go, they thank you.

†

Advice by Father Sergius Bulgakov (from Father John of Kronstadt):

Do not let the celebration of religious services, even the daily ones, become a matter of routine. Always celebrate them with devotion.

Prepare carefully for the Liturgy (this preparation may be spread out over the whole day before).

Do not lift your eyes during the service.

Avoid behaving like an actor.

Do not close your door to anyone, whoever he may be.

Do not refuse money (pride).

†

Hear each person's confession as if it were his last confession before death.

†

The priest listens to heart-rending confessions, listens to them with complete sympathy, and at the same time does not grow exhausted, does not break down under this avalanche of human sin and sorrow: for—thanks to the grace of priesthood—the weight of it all does not fall upon his heart. Thus must we live.

†

Beside parishes and a communal Church life we need what they called 'the small church' in ancient Russia. This means little centres of Church warmth, small shrines belonging to individual families, where people can achieve a close communion with each other, impossible in large parishes with mixed and changing congregations. The duty of the priest is to direct such groups, whose aims may vary: study of the Gospel or of the liturgical services, care of the sick and the poor. Even these goals are not as important as the communication of men with one another. It is difficult even to imagine how many people live among us who are lonely and withdraw from contact with others because of their loneliness.

†

When I work out what I am going to say, there nearly always arises in my mind a genuinely creative process of theological reflection and verbal expression, and the sermon itself is a reproduction of it. This means that the creative process should itself be performed aloud, in front of people. But there are two conditions: a full heart and complete simplicity.

In order to speak without previous preparation, one must keep in mind a precise theme, divided according to the essential ideas. But the real creation must take place during the actual sermon; otherwise, one is burnt out during the preparation, and offers one's listeners only cold ashes.

†

Look for an occasion in a sermon or in general conversation to examine the typical 'stumblings' and 'domestic heresies' which afflict the majority of those who come to confession. Here are some which are particularly widespread: one should not fear God; the primacy of morals; the saints are egoists; denial of fasting;

denial of the Old Testament; prayer at home is better than prayer in Church.

†

The adepts of Christian Science reproach us Orthodox for lack of faith, and for being unable to overcome our illnesses through spiritual forces. Their argument: Christ has made us free from the law of death (Rom. viii. 2).

What shall we say to this?

The gift of healing possessed by the Christians is not a gift of power and divine command over nature . . .

The Apostles themselves were stricken with ailments, many saints (for example St. Ambrose) suffered to the end of their lives from ailments which could not be cured.

This is explained by the fact that, whilst we live in 'this body of death', we must bear all the consequences—until the universal restoration of all things: 'always bearing about in the body the dying of the Lord Jesus' (2 Cor. iv. 10).

†

Outline for a lecture on suffering.[1]

1. The fact of the innocent sufferings of the righteous.

2. Texts from the Gospels: 'the narrow way', 'these are they which came out of great tribulation', 'in the world ye shall have tribulation'.

3. Types of suffering:
   (a) due to sin: 'tribulation and anguish, upon every soul of man that doeth evil' (Rom. ii. 9).
   (b) the denial of oneself—the Cross.
   (c) the refusal to conform to the world.

4. Participation in the sufferings of Christ.

---

[1] Written in pencil, shortly before death.

5. The building up of Christ's body in the world—through the acceptance of Christ and the transfiguration of self.

†

For a funeral sermon: the thought of the frailty of all that is exalted, and of the solidity of all that is gross and earthly, and of resurrection as the finale of this tragedy.

†

Subject for a funeral address: our usual feeling that this world alone exists is complete unbelief in the 'kingdom of heaven'. Hence our sorrow for the dead, which in its foundation is paganism and godlessness. It is necessary to enter into the Christian sense of the reality of the kingdom of heaven.

†

Thoughts for a funeral sermon: Our suffering, pain and tears are understandable; we are so closely linked to our dead—their body is our body; and now this body is stricken with corruption, dies, is turned into earth. In our souls, too, we are one with their being; and suddenly, a part of this is torn away from us, leaves us. How can we help suffering in body and soul?

But there is another solution: the soul, having left its body, is in a troubled, confused, sorrowful condition, however just it may have been upon earth. The very separation from the body is a painful process. On the other hand, the dead have a direct awareness and vision of spiritual realities, the attack of demons, etc. Our sorrow, confusion, tears, and sometimes despair, increase the trouble of their own soul. For this soul of theirs is still very near to us, it is still one with us, and if, during its life in the body, it was not always aware of the psychological state of those who were dear to it, yet now it is particularly defenceless against our despair, which increases its confusion. That is why our duty to the dead is to help them by establishing in ourselves a spirit of prayer, of harmonious and luminous vibration, which penetrates to them also.

Every death is a lesson to us who remain behind; it is a miracle, like the miracle of birth: 'How is it that we are given up to corruption?';[1] it is a reminder of our own approaching death, and when we draw up our plan of life, we too must be oriented towards death. *Respice finem.*

†

To the relatives of the dead, you must speak of the Resurrection of Christ. Advise them to read about Resurrection in the Gospels, and about the wanderings of the soul of the dead, of its tragic condition; about the necessity for the relatives to pray for the deceased. This takes the mind off selfish sorrow, and stops them thinking about the corpse of the dead person (this question troubles many people).

†

After the *Panikhida*, pray for a short time in silence, asking God to fortify and console 'those who stand by and pray'.[2]

†

Subject for a Christmas sermon: the joy of believing in a miracle and meditating upon it, as contrasted with the horror and gloom of having to admit that the laws of nature are immovable.

†

---

[1] Words sung at the Orthodox funeral service.
[2] A phrase used in the service (on the *Panikhida*, see above, p. 41, n. 1).

Subject at a service for the Blessing of the Waters:[1] the nearness of God, of the Holy Spirit, and of His beneficial actions—manifested not only in prayer but in all our pure, disinterested joys, even in the joys springing from the material things of this world — bread, holy oil, and the purest of all elements, water. The consecration of houses, objects, and so forth, is not magic, for Orthodoxy is a religion of complete freedom, and in such cases God's grace, descending on a house, awaits a movement of our heart going out to meet it; that is why we hear in the prayers, recited during the ceremony, an appeal to repentance. To turn to God and to pray together—this is the best way to solve all problems and difficulties.

†

For the second time I have performed the ceremony of receiving a person into the Orthodox Church. I must take note of the following for future occasions.

1. Give in advance to the person to be received the written text of the words which he must say, and explain each point to him.

2. He must learn at least the Creed and he must know the Liturgy, the morning and evening prayers.

3. He should make a general confession from childhood on.

4. Make a religious solemnity of the occasion, especially if it is a young person. I have twice missed this excellent opportunity. The ritual is most impressive. Many would benefit by hearing it and renewing it in their hearts and memory.

†

---

[1] The Great Blessing of the Waters is performed on 6 January (the Feast of the Epiphany) in commemoration of Christ's baptism in the Jordan. Lesser blessings of the waters are performed at other times (e.g. the beginning of the new ecclesiastical year on 1 September). The water hallowed at these services is used by the priest to bless the homes of his parishioners, icons, and other objects.

The symbolism of marriage, taken as a subject for a wedding sermon: the exchange of rings—eternity, everything in common; candles—a bright burning of the soul; the satin carpet underfoot—a common destiny; crowns—a sign of victory, a reward for chastity before wedlock, and a reminder of the crown of martyrs; drinking from the same cup, walking in procession round the church—eternity, etc.[1]

†

Explanation of the Miracle of Cana in Galilee, taken as a symbol: water, representing everyday life, is turned into the wine of joy and creativeness, into something extraordinary, through the mutual love of husband and wife.

Everyone serves the best wine first, and then it gets worse and worse. Such is the law of this world, the law of 'progress'. The child, who has the likeness of an angel, acquires, when it grows up, traits of coarseness, falsehood, the taste of evil. . . . Its simple, wholesome nature, having passed through school and university, through life, loses all the marks of its original integrity, displaying instead complexity, falseness, cowardliness. Such also is the history of nations. Such is likewise the case with the majority of marriages. In the beginning there is a mutual drawing together, a facility of communion with each other; but this is followed by dullness, indifference, boredom, or—still worse—by irritation, often hatred, and even a final break.

But the laws of the Kingdom are different. Water, a natural,

---

[1] Here Father Alexander refers to the different ceremonies in the Orthodox Marriage service:

1. The priest blesses the rings and gives them to bride and groom, who then exchange the rings.
2. Bride and groom hold candles.
3. They both stand on a special carpet.
4. Crowns are blessed and placed on their heads by the priest.
5. They drink from a common cup.
6. Finally they walk together in procession behind the priest.

simple element, is transformed into something higher, into the material of the Eucharist. So it is also with marriage. In its natural state, it is not evil, but simply human. We must take care not to degrade it to a lower level; and we must strive, on the other hand, to attain a genuine communion of spirit, so as to be not only 'one in body', but 'one in soul', making our marriage a reflection of the marriage between Christ and the Church. We must *create* our marriage.

†

Theme for a sermon on marriage.

There are three enemies of a normal family life:

Disillusion with one another—due to blind idealization during the time of engagement.

Pride, treating the other party as one's private property.

Boredom.

May the festive joy of today last all your life, may triviality and boredom never enter it, may you remain, every day of your entire life, new and unusual in each other's eyes. There is but one way to achieve this: a deep spiritual life in each of you. Work hard to develop your own personality, take an interest in other people, study the Word of God, educate and train yourselves.

†

Subject for a sermon to communicants.

Three paths lead from the Holy Supper.

Christ chose the path of ascetic struggle, of suffering, death and resurrection.

The Apostles slept in the Garden of Gethsemane.

Judas chose betrayal, despair, perdition.

†

Some advice on the teaching of religion:

Modern children (especially boys) are difficult material for the teacher of religion to handle. They are bent on reasoning, at an early age they lose creative spontaneity, they have a poorly developed imagination, are sober and practical, inclined to scepticism and mockery. The aesthetic sense is feebly developed, as well as a whole complex of feelings—there is no feeling of reverence in them, no sense of mystery, of hierarchical order. This is why it would be a great mistake to reduce the teaching of religion to the memorizing of certain facts.

The teacher must give first place to the educative aspects, to the process of drawing the children into the realm of religious experience, of implanting religious habits in them. A part of the lesson must always be spent in conversation on moral and religious subjects. Thanks to this discussion, the teacher will be able to learn about the child's prayers at home, about his visits to church, and whether he succeeds in applying to life the lessons in faith and behaviour received at school. Only in this way will religious study cease to be a mere 'period' of class-work, and will become a vivid spiritual task, a *living* experience for the child.

Prayer during lessons on religion is the most important element in this teaching. At the same time, it is a way of repeating the prayers which have been learned, changing them according to circumstances—an approaching feast-day, a holy day, Lent, sickness, a happy or sad event.

An important method of awakening moral and religious emotions in children is to offer them the chance of performing a definite task. Possible forms: looking after the school icon, decorating it with flowers, lighting the lamp, acting as server in the Church services, collecting money for the poor, a special album of Bible illustrations. Forms of interior spiritual activity: prayer for the sick, self-training in order to develop obedience, patience, truthfulness, etc., preparation for confession and communion.

During the lesson, all the Gospel stories must be read in class from the actual Book of the Gospels (and not from text-books). The Gospel Book must be in the hands of all the children, and at the end of the school year, they must know exactly what it contains, the order of the various parts; the pupil must be able to look up the stories he has learned.

It is very important that the course as a whole should follow the cycle of the services in the Church's Year and the Church Calendar, so that the children can then attend services after being prepared for them by the teacher. This is one of the most effective methods of making the practice of religion vivid and active.

The Practical Value of Faith
(A draft)

THIS discussion is intended for unbelievers and is concerned with what religion can give, looking at the matter from *their* materialistic point of view. This is a matter of no interest to believers—they receive the fruits of faith as a result, and not as an end in itself.

Religion is a fact implanted empirically in human nature, and so it does not need to be confirmed by such a temporary and relative phenomenon as European science of the present decade. But as our lives all depend to a considerable extent on the situation in the world around us, and as, amongst other things, we are all affected by science, many people take an interest in this question.

The educated society of Europe has long ago forsaken its churches. Protestantism was the first step taken in this direction. There was a militant period of impiety and mutual struggle. Then followed indifference. Chekhov wrote to Diaghilev: 'I have cast off my faith long ago, and I am puzzled when I see educated people who are believers.' But even such an opinion is already long out of date. Europe has gone through the stage of being afraid of religion, the stage of domination by materialistic and positivistic theories. It has drifted so far away from religion that it has become capable of turning back once more and studying religion from the outside, as an objective fact among other facts.

Nowadays, religion is an object of study for science, a study accompanied by experiments made according to the most modern scientific methods, with deductions, theories, discoveries. And here scientific thought makes for itself a series of discoveries:

1. *The history of culture.* The discovery of a rich religious culture in primitive people. 'All culture comes from the Church' (Frazer). Religion is 'a rich source'. 'Superstitions' are the root from which have sprung the power of the State, property, marriage, respect for the individual, all the arts and all the sciences. 'The most interesting and most precious element in man are his ideals and beliefs. This can also be applied to nations and historical epochs' (James).

Religious fermentation is the symptom of life in a society, and the sign of rich harvests in all its branches.

2. *Psychology.* As the study of religious psychology shows, religion is a conception which gives us an aim in life, an educational method. Discipline of attention in prayer. Rhythm. Ritual—the organization of emotions and affections (mourning).

3. *Psychiatry.* The harm done by egotism. Egocentricity—a fundamental phenomenon of psychopathology. The value of something objective as a means of coming out of onself; enthusiasm, idealization. The placing of the centre of one's soul in a safe place. 'I feel someone's powerful and sweet presence'; 'God surrounds me as a physical atmosphere. He is closer to me than my own breath' (James).

Therapy—the link between religion and nervous disorders.

Neurosis results from the repression of emotions. Confession helps from the medical point of view, by effecting a discharge of emotions (Freud and his school). Through religion egocentricity and solipsism are overcome. Love serves as an anchor planted in the objective. Egoism as a source of illness. 'Fear—the fundamental phenomenon of psychopathology.' 'Idealism—a physiological factor.' 'Peace of heart—the only panacea.'

The testimony of a doctor: 'I told my patient to go to confession, and the mysterious fits which three months of water cure were unable to cure disappeared after one hour of confession.'

'Joy is the best medicine for every neurosis.' 'Religion is the best prophylaxis.' The practical character of religion, the value of saintliness, the harm of sin. To go mad means losing one's axis, revolving in a world of solipsism. The remedies are prayer, God, love, the sense of something objective.

Thus we see how non-religious Europe has rediscovered Christianity, finding in it a powerful prophylactic method.

A Talk Before Confession

'BEHOLD, now is the accepted time; behold, now is the day of salvation' (2 Cor. vi. 2). Now is the time for us to lay aside the heavy burden of sin, to break its chains, and to behold once more the 'fallen and shattered tabernacle' of our soul, renewed and radiant. But the way which leads to this blessed purification is far from easy.

We have not yet begun to prepare for confession, and already our soul hears the voices of temptation: 'Should I put it off? Am I sufficiently prepared, am I not making these special fasts and acts of preparation[1] too often?' We must firmly resist these doubts. 'If thou comest to serve the Lord, prepare thy soul for temptation' (Ecclesiasticus ii. 1). If you have decided to make this special act of preparation, you must expect to encounter many obstacles, interior and exterior; but they vanish as soon as you show firmness in your intentions.

Let us look more specifically at the question of frequent confession. We should go to confession far more often than is customary, and at least during the four Fasts.[2] We who are possessed by 'the slumber of laziness' and inexperienced in penitence, must first learn over and over again how to repent. And secondly, it is necessary to stretch out a thread from one confession to another, so that the interval between each act of special preparation should be filled with a spiritual struggle, with an effort nourished by the

[1] Here the Russian word is *govenie* (see p. 68, n. 2).
[2] In the Orthodox Church, besides the Great Fast of Lent (before Easter), there are three other periods of fasting: before the Feast of the Apostles Peter and Paul (29 June), before the Feast of the Assumption (15 August), and before Christmas.

memory of our previous confession and stimulated by the expectation of the next confession drawing near.

Another difficult question concerns the spiritual director: to whom should you turn? Must you cling to the same director at all costs? May you change your confessor, and if so, in what circumstances? Priests experienced in the spiritual life assert that you should not change, even if he is only your confessor, not your spiritual director. True, it sometimes happens that after a successful confession, the next one, heard by the same priest, is uninspiring and produces only a feeble reaction; then the thought of changing his confessor occurs to the penitent. But this is no reason for taking such a serious step. Quite apart from the fact that our personal feelings during confession do not affect the essence of the sacrament, the absence of any spiritual feeling during confession is sometimes the sign of our own spiritual apathy. John of Kronstadt says of this state: 'Penitence must be free, not forced by the confessor.' If a man is really plagued by his sin, it makes no difference through whom he confesses this painful sin; all he wants is to confess it as soon as possible and to find relief. It is another thing if we go to confession just in order to talk to someone, leaving aside the essence of the sacrament. We must distinguish between confession and a spiritual talk, which can be conducted outside the sacrament. It is better for such a talk to take place separately, for conversation—even on spiritual topics—may distract the penitent and fill him with a certain coldness, leading him into theological discussions and diminishing the fervour of his repentance.

Confession is not just a talk about your faults and doubts, it is not a way of telling your confessor all about yourself, and least of all is it a 'pious practice'. Confession is an act of fervent, heartfelt repentance, a thirst for purification; it springs from an awareness of what is holy, it means dying to sin and coming alive again to sanctity. Contrition is in itself already a measure of sanctity. Insensibility and unbelief mean that we are outside sanctity, outside God.

Let us examine what our attitude should be toward the sacrament of repentance, what is demanded from one who seeks this sacrament, how to prepare for it, what is to be considered as the most important moment, in that part of the sacrament which concerns the penitent.

(1) Undoubtedly, the first act will be *a searching of the heart*. That is why the days of preparation have been instituted. 'To see your sins, in all their multiplicity and hideousness—this is indeed a gift of God,' writes John of Kronstadt. People inexperienced in the spiritual life usually see neither the number of their sins nor their 'hideousness'. 'Nothing in particular', 'like everyone else', 'only petty sins', 'I have neither stolen nor killed': such is the usual beginning of confession by many penitents. And what about pride, refusal to suffer reproaches, hardness of heart, sycophancy, weakness of faith and love, faint-heartedness, spiritual sloth, are not these serious sins? Can we assert that we love God sufficiently, that our faith is active and fervent? That we love every man as our brother in Christ? That we have attained meekness, freedom from anger, humility? If not, what does our Christianity amount to? How shall we explain our self-confidence during confession if not by 'petrified insensibility', by the 'spiritual death which precedes our bodily death'? Why did the Holy Fathers, who left us their penitential prayers, consider themselves the worst of sinners and cry out with profound conviction to the most sweet Jesus: 'Nobody, from the beginning of time, has sinned as I, wicked and profligate, have sinned!' And we are convinced that all goes well with us! The more brightly the light of Christ shines in our hearts, the clearer grows the awareness of our faults, ulcers, and wounds. And, conversely, people plunged in the darkness of sin see nothing in their hearts; and even if they see, they are not horrified, for they have no standard of comparison.

This is why the shortest way to attain a knowledge of our sin is to draw nearer to the light and to pray for that light which judges the world and all that is 'worldly' in ourselves (John iii. 19).

As long as we lack that closeness to Christ which makes the feeling of repentance our habitual condition, we must prepare for confession by an examination of conscience according to the commandments, by certain prayers (for instance the third of the evening prayers, the fourth of the prayers before communion), and by texts from Scripture (for instance, Romans v. 12, Ephesians iv, and James, especially chapter iii).

When examining your soul's economy you should try to distinguish the basic sins from those that are derived from them, symptoms from deeper causes. For instance, distraction in prayer, drowsiness and inattention in church, absence of interest in reading the Holy Scriptures are certainly very serious; but are not these sins derived from lack of faith and a weak love of God? We must make ourselves realize our own self-will, disobedience, self-justification, refusal to accept reproaches, to make concessions, our obstinacy; but it is still more important to discover how these sins are linked with self-love and pride. If we are aware of being too socially inclined, too talkative, too ready to make fun of things, too much concerned with our outward appearance, and not only with our own, but also with that of our family and with the external arrangement of our home—we should examine carefully whether this is not a sign of 'many-sided vanity'. If we take our misfortunes too much to heart, suffer too deeply from separation, bewail the departed and find no comfort, then, setting aside the intensity of our emotions, does not this prove our lack of faith in Divine Providence?

There is also another helpful method bringing us to the knowledge of our sins—to recall what we are most often accused of by other people, especially by those who live near us, by our family. Their reproaches, attacks and accusations are nearly always well founded.

Before confession it is also necessary to ask forgiveness of all those whom we have offended, and so to go to confession with a clear conscience.

During such an examination of conscience we must take care not to indulge in an exaggerated scrupulousness and petty suspiciousness concerning every movement of our heart; if we give way to this tendency we may easily lose the power to discriminate between the important and the unimportant, and become lost in matters of detail. In that case, you should interrupt for a time the examination of conscience and, following a plain but wholesome spiritual diet, simplify and clarify your soul with prayer and good deeds.

Preparation for confession does not consist in recalling your sins as fully as possible and even writing them down. It means striving to attain such a state of concentration, seriousness, and prayer that your sins will become as clear as if they had been exposed to the light. In other words, you should bring to your confessor not a list of sins but a feeling of repentance, not a minutely studied dissertation but a contrite heart.

(2) But to know your sins does not yet mean to *repent* of them. True, our Lord accepts a sincere, conscientious confession even though it is not accompanied by a feeling of repentance (if we courageously confess as well this sin of 'petrified insensibility'). However, *contrition of the heart*, sorrow for our sins, is the most important thing that we can bring to confession. But what are we to do if our heart, 'dried up with sin', is not watered by the vivifying stream of tears? What if 'weakness of soul and frailty of body' are so great that we are incapable of sincere repentance? All the same, this is no reason for putting off confession—God may touch our heart during the confession itself; the very confession, the naming of our sins, may soften our heart, refine our spiritual sight, sharpen the feeling of repentance. More than anything else, our spiritual sloth can be overcome with the help of the preparation before confession: fasting which exhausts the body, breaking down our sense of physical well-being and complacency—things fatal to spiritual life—prayer, nightly meditation on death, reading from the Gospels, from the Lives of the Saints and of the works

of the Holy Fathers, an intensified struggle with self, and the practice of good deeds. Our insensibility during confession is usually rooted in the lack of fear of God and in a secret unbelief. That is where our efforts should be centred. And that is why our tears at confession are so important—they soften our petrified condition, they shake us 'from top to bottom'. They confer on us simplicity and self-forgetfulness, and remove the main obstacle to confession—our sense of 'self'. The proud, the vain do not weep. Once you begin to weep, it means that your heart is softened, melted, has humbled itself. That is why, after such tears, meekness, freedom from anger, a softening of the heart, tenderness, and peace of soul are granted to those whom God has sent these 'joy-creating' tears. We should not be ashamed of tears during confession, we should let them flow freely, washing away our iniquities. 'Grant me rivers of tears on this great day of Lent, that I may weep and wash away my iniquities, born of seduction, and I shall stand before Thee purified.'[1]

(3) The third stage of repentance is the *oral confession of sins*. Do not wait to be questioned, make an effort for yourself; confession is a courageous feat of self-constraint. You must speak with precision, without veiling the ugliness of sin by vague expressions (as, for instance, 'I have sinned against the seventh commandment'). It is very difficult in confession to avoid the temptation of self-justification: we try to put before the confessor 'extenuating circumstances', and make allusions to a 'third person' who led us into sin. All this is a mark of vanity, indicating the absence of deep repentance and a continued stagnation in sin. Sometimes penitents excuse themselves by pleading a faulty memory which prevents them from recalling a sin. True, we often forget our trespasses. But is this due only to a weak memory? We remember for years on end certain occasions when our pride was specially wounded or, conversely, specially flattered. We recall for

---

[1] From a hymn sung during the first week of Lent.

many years the praise we received. We can remember distinctly and for a long time everything which made a deep impression on us. If we forget our sins, does this not mean that we do not attach a serious meaning to them?

As a sign that we have achieved real repentance, we experience a sense of lightheartedness, of purity and inexpressible joy, in which sin seems to us as difficult and impossible to commit, as this joy seemed to us unattainable only a short time before.

Our repentance will not be complete unless we resolve at the same time in our innermost heart not to return to the sin we have confessed. But you may say: how is this possible? How can I promise to myself and to my confessor that I will not repeat this sin? Is not the opposite nearer to the truth—the certainty that the sin will be repeated? Each of us (so we argue) knows from experience that after a certain time we return inevitably to the same sins. As we watch ourselves from year to year we see no progress whatever—we jump, and yet find ourselves again at the same spot. It would be terrible if this were really the case. But fortunately it is not so. Provided we genuinely desire to correct our faults, successive confessions and communions never fail to produce a salutary change in our soul. The fact is that, after all, we are not our own judges; a man cannot judge correctly about himself, nor tell whether he has become better or worse, because he who judges and that which he judges are both dimensions that are changing. A growing severity toward ourselves, an increase of spiritual insight, an intensified fear of sin, may create the illusion that our sins have multiplied and grown in force; they have remained as before, or perhaps have weakened, but previously we did not take so much notice of them. Moreover, God's special Providence often closes our eyes to our spiritual progress, in order to protect us from the grave sin of pride and vanity. It often happens that the sin has remained, but frequent confession and the reception of the holy sacraments have weakened and shaken its roots. And the struggle itself with sin, the suffering we endure because of our sins, is this not an acquisition? St. John of the Ladder says: 'Do not be afraid, even though you fall every day, so long as you do not depart from the ways of God; stand courageously and the angel who guards you will respect your patience.'

If there is no feeling of relief, of renewal, you must find the strength to return to confession, to cleanse your soul entirely from impurities, to wash away its blackness and iniquity with tears. He who strives always finds what he seeks.

Only let us not ascribe our progress to *ourselves*, regarding it as something that depends on *our* strength, placing our hopes on *our* efforts. This would be to destroy all that we have gained. 'Gather together my distracted mind, O Lord, and cleanse my icy heart; grant me repentance as Thou didst to Peter, grant me sighs of contrition like the publican's, and tears like the harlot's.'

A Retreat in a Monastery[1]

O LORD, this climb will never end! Instead of a path—the dry bed of a torrent, covered with round pebbles which slip underfoot. All round the forest has been felled, only the bristle of low bushes remains. Now, at last, there is a mountain pass. The way winds along the slope of the hill and I can hear the rustling of thick woods. Nothing is comparable to the joy experienced on a mountain pass; you climb endlessly uphill, ahead you see rocks and behind you the misty valley recedes far below. You are tired out, you plod on mechanically, no longer seeing anything: and then suddenly, the ascent ends, the mountain breeze blows in your face, the path winds downhill, and a limitless blue horizon unfolds before your eyes.

I felt slightly dizzy and my heart beat faster when the downward path came to an end and I saw the entrance before me—two round stone towers, covered with moss and crumbling at the top.

It was strange for me to come alone. I had often visited this place with a noisy group of friends; we entered laughing, demanded tea and chatted idly with the monks. Now I had come with a request, hoping for something. And everything looked different.

I threw my things down on a table near a tall ash-tree, where we usually drank tea, and I remained there waiting. They had already seen me—a monk with an enormous black beard was coming towards me.

'Alexander, my dear, at last you have come!' He spoke with a

---

[1] Notes written by Father Alexander during his schooldays. The monastery he describes lay in Georgia, in the Caucasus. The Georgians still speak their own native tongue, which is not of Slavonic origin.

strong Georgian accent and there was a bright smile on his face. 'Come along with me, here is your cell.' We made our way to a stone building beside the church. Father Jonas opened the door of a small, damp room with a vaulted ceiling and niches in the stone walls.

The days flew by. They were outwardly monotonous, but as light and refreshing as the cold, sun-drenched air of these mountains.

I woke early—about five o'clock. I washed quickly and ran to the corner tower at the east; the wet grass was cold and pricked my feet like tiny icicles. Then I climbed straight along the wall which was crumbling and overgrown with grass, till I reached the round tower. At my feet, just beyond the wall, there grew a beech-wood, the tops of the trees coming up to the very edge of the wall. The trees descended in terraces to the blue stream of the Aragva flowing between grey sandbanks. Further off, the dark, wooded mountain ranges, veiled in the morning mist, loomed higher and higher; and above them, higher still, as if resting on the clouds, glistened the snowcapped peaks of the main Caucasian ranges. There were so many of them that I had to turn my gaze along the horizon from east to west, to take them all in.

The shadow of the old ash-trees still lay across the small court, moist with dew, and we were already drinking tea in the veranda built against the wall. Father Jonas took a rather dirty red handkerchief (which he called a table cloth) and spread it over the wooden, weather-beaten table; he produced some clay mugs, decorated with a pattern of trees and riders, and brought a loaf of brownish-mauve bread, streaked with mildew; it was tasteless and dry like earth (they baked it once a month and kept it in the church). The sun was shining, reflected on the samovar and on the mugs, and shed its warmth through the thin trellis of the veranda, while we drank our tea unsweetened, taking small bites of sugar, and 'held sweet converse together', to use Father Jonas' expression.

A year ago, a band of brigands broke into the monastery; they threw the Superior, Father Jonas, off a rock into the snow. The fall damaged his hip and he is afflicted with rheumatism which has bent him in two. Now Father Jonas looks like an old man; his tanned face is covered with a net of wrinkles, he can scarcely move and never feels really warm. He knows that he will soon die and unconcernedly showed me the place where he will be buried. The 'world' he views with intense exasperation. 'Are there any monks today?' he said. 'They put a mitre on their head, ride in a carriage, their belly is that big.'[1] On the other hand he thinks very highly of his monastery: 'See for yourself, we live like the hermits of the desert. Our water supply is down there, at the foot of the hill, a mile away. That is as it should be, according to the rules—a monk must work.'

Father John—less formally, Ivane—listened respectfully to Father Jonas, his Superior. Ivane was gayer—alert and active.

After the morning tea, I read the Gospels, sitting on the stones, turning my back to the sun—it was never warm here. I helped Father Jonas in the kitchen garden—a small plot of land clinging to the rocks, wrested with a great struggle from the forest. The beds were all on a slope and the earth was mixed with pebbles. We weeded and put up stakes for the beans. I looked at Father Jonas; his stooping figure, black skull-cap and dark purple cassock were silhouetted against the rows of stakes. At noon, we had dinner. We ate boiled beans and the black bread; sometimes there was sheep-cheese, sharp and rich.

It is getting warmer. Father Jonas is taking a nap on the lumber stacked near the church. Father John has stepped out onto the balcony of his cell and starts mending his own brown habit. I go for a walk in the woods. I would like to find the rock which I saw on my way to the monastery. There were many caves. Eagles must be nesting in them.

---

[1] Only monks can become bishops in the Orthodox Church. On their appointment they leave their monastic community and reside at the see of their diocese. Father Jonas evidently considers their way of life too worldly and luxurious.

It is good to be in the woods. The pale trunks of the beaches are tightly encased in their bark; beneath the branches the earth is strewn with leaves, like the expensive flooring in some palatial home. Long shoots of ivy entwine the tree-trunks with leathery leaves that have an artificial look. Further on some bright red flowers are growing on the slope of a ravine. What strange plants they are: a straight, fleshy, violet stalk is covered with fine violet scales or leaves, and a fiery flower crowns it. It gives an impression of something poisonous and secret.

The sun has turned westward. Everything is veiled with a light mist. It must be hot there, down below, but visibility is good. The Kura glints dully among the dark patches of the woods, and the hills rise above it in terraces. Below, at the foot of our hill, right by the precipice, the yellow wall and the towers of our monastery of the Holy Cross stand out at the very spot where

> *Embracing each other like two sisters,*
> *The streams of the Aragva and the Kura meet.*[1]

The sun is already low as I return. Its rays are quite yellow and long warm shadows stretch across the valley.

In my cell, I decorate the niche with ivy and place a flat cup with flowers in front of the icon.

In the evening I go to fetch water. The spring is far below. It is enclosed in hewn stones, and an ice-cold jet spouts from it. It is a little uncanny here. Everything is so silent among the old beeches, and the path strewn with yellow leaves is so quiet.

I hear someone's steps. The figures of three men emerge at the end of the path—probably charcoal burners. Covered with coal-dust, their bearded, peasant faces have a fiendish look, and their eyes are red from smoke. 'Gamardjoba':[2] one of them greets me and takes off his round cap. I bow and answer: 'Gagimardjos.'[2] They pass by me, their loose shoes of hide shuffling out of step. One of

---

[1] From a poem by Lermontov.   [2] A greeting in Georgian.

the men lags behind; he puts down his belongings, tied up in a red handkerchief, close to the spring and bends over my pail. Then he thanks me for the drink and catches up with his companions. I climb up the hill with my pail. Half-way up I stop to rest near a small wooden chapel; it contains the icon of a local saint who lived in our monastery: St. John of Zedazeny, with a wolf. The names of visitors are carved on the walls and wooden benches. There is a bouquet of dried wild flowers on the floor.

And now I enter the monastery as one of the family, passing through the gates which before admitted me merely as a guest. I feel deeply grateful to these moss-covered towers rooted in the rock, to the silence of the green courtyard which seems to unfold and open wide after the dark path of the forest.

Just as I enter, a small bell rings in the tower. It is such an unexpected sound in this isolated mountain dwelling. It rings again and again: today is Saturday. But how strange to hear this bell on the top of a bare mountain—nobody will hear it, nobody will come. The very aimlessness of this tolling makes it more moving, more significant.

Father John emerges from his cell, solemn, austere, quite different from the Ivane who worked with his hoe in the vegetable garden there below and chatted gaily with me about trivial matters.

Father Jonas also goes into the church, and I enter it after him. In the narthex there are frescoes, crudely painted: red, orange and blue are the dominant colours. The church is cold and dark; the stone walls are bare and the new, low wooden iconostasis seems made of cardboard, by contrast with the heavy architecture of the church.

I go to the back of the church, behind a pillar, trying not to make any noise: but even the slight scraping of my soles on the stone floor echoes loudly in every corner and under the vault. Father John officiates, while Father Jonas takes the parts of the deacon, reader and choir. They are the only two monks who are left in the monastery. Father Jonas chants rapidly, in a loud, high-pitched voice, cracked and elderly; it fills the church with echoes which interfere with and interrupt each other. I stand behind the square pillar. From time to time, at a sign from Father Jonas, I light the censer and hand it to him, then once more go back to my place. I am slightly bored, because the service is conducted in the old Georgian language, and I do not understand anything. Had it been in Russian, I would have listened avidly and would have remembered the prayers. But here I am bored, I even dream of some hot tea. But there, we have come to the end: how unexpectedly they have finished the service. We go out of the church. It is cold outside. I am alone at the door of my cell; automatically I turn my head to the north where, deep down in the valley, the lights of the distant city glow, tremble and shimmer. It is hard to believe that in that far-away, sparkling point of light, people live and walk about, that my family is there. In the dining-room at the large, white table, under the lamp, mother is pouring tea, while in the next room my brother is playing the *Apassionata*.

The night is falling. It is cold. The light of the moon creeps along the wall. Now it grows paler: a cloud of mist floats above the church, almost sweeping its roof. Another cloud floats nearby, enveloping for a moment the old ash-trees on the edge of the precipice. The city is also hidden, then emerges once more deep down in the valley. . . .

I am not there with you, and you are not visible either; there is only that sparkling circle of light in the valley. If you were all dying at this moment, I would not feel it.

A long time ago, one night in the early spring, I was washing photographic plates under the tap in the dark kitchen. The water was so cold, and there was a spot of moonlight on the wall, near the running water; from time to time the moonlight fell on my wet hands and glistened on the plate. I shuddered. I suddenly had a foretaste of that sadness, there on the mountain, flooded with moonlight, of my solitude there, and the cold. It was then that I decided to come here. But now that I have actually gone away, that

I am really far from everyone, my solitude is different and I am glad to be here.

Here I am in my cell. The candle, fixed on the table, lights up the stone wall, but does not reach up to the dark vaults. I write and read, wrapped in my sheepskin cape. It is late. I blow out the candle, and the vigil-light in the niche in front of the icon glows more brightly. I try not to tread on the slab of stone marking the tomb of some archimandrite,[1] who is buried here. The slab is always cold and it seems to me that this cold spreads throughout the room.

Silently I recite the prayers of intercession. A phase of inattention crosses my mind—then I return again to the words of the prayer.

I go up to the open window and peer into the damp darkness. Everything is shrouded in dark blue-green shadows; a billowing cloud of mist spreads over the valley, cutting it in two. It is still and quiet.

---

[1] A title of honour given to priest-monks of senior rank.

The Devil's Stronghold
(On Pride)

ISAAC the Syrian—who knew, as no one else, the depths of the spirit of man—wrote in his forty-first Instruction:

'He who knows his own sin is higher than the man who resurrects the dead by his prayers. He who has been granted the gift of seeing himself is superior to the man who sees the angels.'

The examination of the theme which we have chosen for our title leads precisely to this self-knowledge.

Pride, self-esteem, vanity, to which we may add haughtiness, arrogance, conceit—all these are various aspects of one basic phenomenon: *concentration on self*. Let us use this last phrase as a general term to cover all the sins we have just mentioned.

Among them all, there are two which stand out: vanity and pride. According to the *Ladder*, they are like a youth and a grown man, like seed and wheat, the beginning and the end.

What are the symptoms of this initial sin of vanity? An impatience of any criticism, a thirst for praise, a search for easy ways, constant orientation towards others: 'What will they think?' Vanity sees from afar the prospective spectator; it makes the angry gentle, the frivolous serious, the absent-minded attentive, the greedy abstinent; and so forth. All this lasts as long as there are spectators.

Childish and youthful timidity is often nothing but hidden selfishness and vanity.

This very same orientation toward a spectator explains the sin of self-justification, which often creeps inadvertently even into our confession. 'I have sinned as others do', we say: 'there have been only petty sins, I have killed nobody, I did not steal.' In the diaries of Countess Sophie Tolstoy there is the following characteristic entry: 'I did not know how to educate my children (having married when still a very young girl and after being locked up for eighteen years in the country), and this often tortures me.' The main words of repentance are completely obliterated by the self-justification in brackets.

The demon of vanity rejoices, writes St. John of the Ladder, when he sees our virtues increase. 'When I fast, I am vain; when I hide my sacrifice and keep it secret, I am vain about my discretion. If I dress well, I am vain, but when I change into poor clothes, I am even more vain. If I speak, I am possessed by vanity; if I observe silence, I am once more given up to vanity. Whichever way we turn these thorns, their spikes will still point upwards.'

Leo Tolstoy knew well the poisonous nature of vanity. In his early diaries he harshly accuses himself of vanity. In one of his diaries of the eighteen-fifties he bitterly complains that as soon as a good feeling arises spontaneously in his soul, it is immediately followed by retrospection, by a self-examination that is full of vanity; and so the most precious movements of the soul disappear, melting like snow in the sun. They melt—in other words, they die. This means that as a result of vanity all that is best in us dies, we kill ourselves through vanity; we replace the true, simple, good life with spectres. The vain man rushes towards death and finds it.

'Rarely have I seen', writes one of our contemporary authors, 'the great silent joy of suffering pass through human souls without being accompanied by its repulsive fellow-traveller—a frivolous and overtalkative affectation (vanity). What is the essence of affectation? To my mind it is the incapacity to *be*. Truly speaking, affected people are non-existent, for they adapt themselves to the opinion of other people about them. When experiencing the greatest sufferings, affected people have an inherent tendency to show off these sufferings to others, for the eyes of others are for them what the limelight is for a theatrical setting' (Stepun, *Nikolay Pereslegin*).[1]

An increasing vanity breeds *pride*.

Pride is extreme self-confidence, together with the rejection of all that is not 'mine'. It leads to anger, to cruelty and spite, to the refusal of God's help. It is 'the demon's stronghold', a 'brazen wall' between ourselves and God (Abba Pimen);[2] it is hostility to God, the beginning of all sin, it is present in every sin. For every sin is a wilful abandonment to one's passion, a conscious breaking of God's law, defiance of God, even though 'the person who is subject to pride is particularly in need of God, for men cannot save him' (*The Ladder*).

From where does this passion stem? How does it start? What does it feed on? What stages does it pass through in its development? By what signs can we recognize it?

The last question is especially important, for the proud man usually does not *see* his sin. A certain wise *starets* during confession urged a brother not to be proud. The brother, blinded in his mind, replied: 'Forgive me, Father, but there is no pride in me.' The wise *starets* then said: 'My child, what better proof could you give of your pride than this answer?'

Certainly, if a man finds it difficult to ask for forgiveness, if he is touchy and suspicious, if he remembers evil and judges others, all this is undoubtedly a symptom of pride.

Symeon the New Theologian writes very well about this: 'If a man suffers greatly in his heart when he is slighted or annoyed, it is clear that such a man bears the ancient serpent (pride) in his bosom. If he suffers offences in silence, he will render this serpent powerless and weak. But if he answers back with bitterness and speaks insolently, he will lend the serpent the strength to instill poison into his heart and cruelly to devour his bowels.'

---

[1] Fedor Stepun (1884–1965), Russian philosopher and writer.
[2] Egyptian hermit of the fifth century.

In the *Sermon to the Pagans* of St. Athanasius the Great we find the following words: 'Men have fallen into self-lust, preferring contemplation of self to the contemplation of God.' In this brief definition the very essence of pride is revealed: man, for whom the centre of desire was originally God, has turned away from Him and 'fallen into self-lust', desiring and loving himself more than God, preferring contemplation of self to the contemplation of the Divine.

In our life, this 'self-contemplation' and 'self-lust' have become our very nature and are manifested, for instance, in a powerful instinct of *self-preservation*, in the life of the body, as well as of the spirit.

As a malignant tumour often starts with a blow or with the continuous irritation of a certain part of the body, so the sickness of pride often starts either with a sudden trauma of the soul (for instance with a great sorrow) or with a prolonged interest in oneself, arising from success, satisfaction, the constant exercise of one's talents.

Often such a person is what we call 'temperamental': he 'lets himself go', he is 'passionate', talented. He is a sort of spouting geyser, and by incessant activity he prevents both God and man from approaching him. He is full of himself, self-absorbed, self-entranced. He sees and feels nothing except his own burning fire, his talent which he enjoys, receiving from it complete happiness and satisfaction. One can hardly do anything with such people, until they have exhausted themselves, until the volcano is extinct. This is the danger of all gifts, of all talent. These qualities must be balanced by a full and profound spiritual life.

In the opposite condition—in the experience of grief—we find the same results: the person is 'absorbed' in his grief, the surrounding world becomes dim and dark for him; he can speak and think of nothing but his sorrow; finally he lives by it, clinging to it as the only thing which remains in his life, its one and only meaning. For there are men 'who have dared to find delight even in the sense of their own humiliation' (Dostoyevsky, *Notes from the Underground*).

Often this self-centredness is developed by quiet, silent, submissive people whose personal life has been frustrated since childhood, and this 'frustrated subjectivity finds compensation in an egocentric tendency' (Jung, *Psychological Types*), which takes the most varied forms: susceptibility, over-scrupulousness, coquettishness, the desire to attract attention even by spreading and exaggerating evil rumours about onself, and finally a psychotic state of fixed ideas, persecution mania or megalomania (Poprishchin in Gogol's story).[1]

So concentration on self leads man away from the world and from God; one might say that he cuts himself off from the common stem of the universe and becomes nothing but a shaving curled around empty space.

Let us try to point out the main landmarks in the development of pride from mild self-satisfaction to extreme spiritual darkening and final destruction.

In the beginning: merely a preoccupation with self, an almost normal condition accompanied by a happy mood which often turns into frivolity. A person is pleased with himself, laughs frequently, whistles, sings, snaps his fingers. He likes to be original, to surprise others with his paradoxes, to be witty; he manifests certain caprices, is fastidious in food. He willingly gives advice, meddling in a friendly way in other people's business. He involuntarily betrays his exceptional interest in himself in such phrases as these (interrupting others): 'Let me tell you', or 'I know a better one', or, 'I am in the habit of . . .', 'The rule I follow is . . .', 'I usually prefer' (in Turgenev).

Speaking of another person's sorrow, he often exclaims unconsciously: 'I was so upset, I cannot get over it!' On the other hand this type of person relies enormously on other people's

---

[1] Poprishchin, the imaginary author of Gogol's short story, *The Memoirs of a Madman*.

approval, and depending on whether it is given or withheld he becomes either radiant or dejected. Generally speaking, however, his mood at this stage is cheerful. This sort of egocentricity is characteristic of youth, though it is found in mature age also.

It is fortunate for man if at this stage he encounters serious worries, especially about others (marriage, a family), work, labour. Or else if he is drawn toward religious life: attracted by the beauty of spiritual effort he will see his own wretchedness and littleness and will desire the help of grace. Unless this happens, the sickness develops further.

Next there appears a sincere belief in one's own superiority, often accompanied by an unchecked flow of words. After all, what is verbosity, if not on the one hand a lack of modesty, and on the other pleasure in a primitive process of self-disclosure? The egoistic character of garrulousness is just as bad even when, as sometimes happens, the flow of words is inspired by a serious topic: the proud man may comment on the virtues of humility and silence; he may praise fasting or discuss whether good works are preferable to prayer.

Self-assurance turns rapidly into a passion for commanding. The proud man encroaches upon the will of others, while not tolerating the slightest encroachment on his own will. He imposes himself upon the attention, time and energy of all around him. He becomes impudent and brazen. His own affairs are important; other people's concerns are of no consequence. He undertakes everything, interferes everywhere.

At this stage the proud man's mood alters. As a result of his aggressiveness he naturally meets opposition and rebuff; he becomes irritable, obstinate, quarrelsome; he is convinced that nobody understands him, not even his spiritual director. His clashes with 'the world' grow sharper, and the proud individual finally makes a choice: his ego sets itself in opposition against men, although not yet against God.

And now his soul becomes dark and cold; arrogance, contempt, anger and hate inhabit it. His mind is obscured, the distinction between good and evil grow confused, for it is replaced by the distinction between 'mine' and 'not mine'. He shirks all obedience; he becomes insufferable in every society; his goal is to pursue his own line, to put people to shame, to shock them; he greedily seeks publicity, even if it is scandalous, taking his revenge on the world which did not recognize him and thus getting his own back. If he is a monk he leaves the monastery, which he can stand no longer, and seeks his own way. At times, this force of self-affirmation is directed toward material ends—a career, political or social activity— and, if the person is talented, it may lead to creative work. In this field, the proud man may win a few victories, thanks to the pressure he exercises. Heresies and schisms also arise on this soil.

Finally, at the last stage, the proud man breaks with God Himself. If he previously sinned out of mischief or mutinousness, he now permits himself every excess; sin no longer worries him, it becomes habitual. If during this period he feels any happiness, he is happy with the devil and along dark roads. The condition of his soul is sombre, closed to the light, his loneliness is complete; at the same time he is sincerely convinced that he has chosen the right path; he feels perfect security, while dark wings whirl him along to destruction.

In fact the condition of such a man can scarcely be distinguished from insanity.

Even in this life, the proud man dwells in almost complete isolation (the darkness of hell). See how he talks and argues; either he does not hear at all what is said to him, or he can only hear what fits his views; if something goes against his opinion, he is as furious as if he had been personally insulted; he answers sarcastically or makes a passionate rebuttal. In those who surround him he sees only the characteristics which he attributes to them; thus even when he praises others, he remains proud, locked in himself, blind to objective truth.

It is typical that the most common forms of mental illness—

megalomania and the persecution complex—are directly derived from 'excessive self-consciousness'; it would be quite impossible to find these defects in the humble, the simple, the self-forgetful. Psychiatrists regard an exaggerated sense of one's own personality, a hostile attitude towards other people, the loss of a normal capacity of adjustment, and distorted judgements as the main causes of insanity (paranoia). The classic paranoiac never criticizes himself, he is always right in his own eyes and bitterly displeased with the people around him and with the conditions of his life.

Thus we come to realize the depth of the definition given by St. John of the Ladder: 'Pride is the extreme poverty of the soul.'

The proud suffers defeat on all fronts.

Psychologically, he suffers from melancholy, darkness, sterility.

Morally, from solitude, the withering of love, malice.

From the theological point of view, from a death of the soul preceding physical death, from hell during this present life.

Epistemologically, from solipsism.

Physiologically and pathologically, from nervous and mental sickness.

In conclusion, we naturally ask ourselves: how shall we fight against this disease, with what shall we oppose the destruction that threatens those who follow this way?

The answer is derived from the very essence of the question. Pride is overcome by humility, by obedience to objective truth, an obedience undertaken in gradual stages: obedience to those we love, to the laws of this world, to objective truth, to beauty, to all that is good in us and outside us, obedience to God's teaching, and finally obedience to the Church, to her commandments, to her sacramental life.

And in order to achieve this humility and obedience, we must undertake that which stands first on the Christian way: 'If any man will come after me, let him deny himself, and take up his cross, and follow me' (Matt. xvi. 24).

Man must deny himself, deny himself every day. Man must

take up his cross 'daily', as the oldest manuscripts have it (Luke ix. 23)—the cross of patiently accepting grievances, choosing the last place, bearing sorrows and illness, the silent acceptance of insults, of full unreserved obedience—immediate, voluntary, joyful, fearless and constant.

Then he will find the way to the realm of peace, of that 'deepest humility which destroys all passions'.

Glory be to God who 'resisteth the proud, and giveth grace to the humble' (1 Peter v. 5).